Wilbur,
Keep shining t

Endorse...

Charles Simpson
(I Cor 15:57)

Charles's relationship with my brother, David Wilkerson, gave him a very privileged opportunity to witness both the man and his ministry. This inspiring story of his spiritual journey tells how, under the teaching and mentoring of, and personal contact with, David Wilkerson, he learned many valuable lessons. I worked with Charles at Times Square Church, as well as at Teen Challenge, and I know firsthand his compassion for the lost, his teaching gifts, and his prayer leadership. I highly recommend this book, especially for young people who desire to be used by God in ministry.

DON WILKERSON
Co-Founder of Teen Challenge & Times Square Church

As a seasoned leader who worked closely with Pastor Dave at Times Square Church, Charles takes us behind the scenes, offering great spiritual insight, helping us to grasp what made this giant of the faith so special. This book was a joy for me to read and to recommend to you!

DR. MICHAEL L. BROWN
Host of *The Line of Fire* Radio Broadcast

When I first met Charles Simpson at a Times Square Church service, he was leading the congregation in prayer. That prayer touched me so deeply that I immediately knew why David Wilkerson chose him to be one of his leaders. Charles has a burden for the lost and a burning desire to see people embrace their divine destiny. This book will touch your heart, as it did mine. His personal mentorship and ministry with David Wilkerson will inspire your faith and compel you to share God's love with the hurting. David Wilkerson's step of faith to share

God's love with hardened gang members has resulted in millions of lives being rescued and restored. Charles captures the very mission of Jesus through this book, and more so through his life as a committed servant-leader at Brooklyn Teen Challenge.

PASTOR JIMMY JACK
Freedom Chapel & Long Island Teen Challenge

From gales of laughter as I read the opening stories, to soul-searching examination as Charles shares some of David Wilkerson's incredible applications of biblical truth, to tears of joy as his family gathered around his mother's deathbed, only to see a miracle...I could not put this book down! It is a beautiful reflection of one of David Wilkerson's most amazing legacies—the spiritual sons into which he poured God's Word through decades of ministry with Teen Challenge, World Challenge, and Times Square Church; sons who continue to carry his burden for souls long after he went home to be with the Lord.

BERNIE GILLOTT
Global Evangelism Coordinator for Global Teen Challenge

Charles Simpson is the perfect person to write this book. Over the many years I have known him, I have seen him personify the lessons he learned from David Wilkerson. Just like his mentor, Charles carries a passion for the broken and a desire to see God's people abandon all moral compromise. David Wilkerson believed God could change the hearts of even the most hardened sinners and worked tirelessly to see this happen. In the same way, I have seen Charles labor with the same sacrificial spirit as he has laid down his life to see God's purposes fulfilled in New York City, one soul at a time. Charles's story not only reflects on the past, but it also challenges the reader to follow the trail blazed by David Wilkerson, paved by heartfelt tears, prevailing prayer, and tenacious faith in Jesus Christ.

PASTOR GARY FISHMAN
Surpassing Glory Ministry
Bronx, New York

David Wilkerson is one of the historic figures in New York City and American Christianity. He embodied bold, redemptive leadership. Charles Simpson has made an important contribution with this work.

Dr. Mac Pier
Founder and CEO, The NYC Leadership Center

This is a fascinating, fresh, and non-idolizing look at the life of David Wilkerson, written from the perspective of a spiritual son. I heard much of what is written here firsthand at FIRE School of Ministry in New York City. Pastor Charles profoundly impacted me while as a pastor, teacher, and mentor, he poured out his heart of fatherly love to all his students. This book challenged and stirred my heart afresh to return to the secret place of seeking the Lord in prayer, being gently reminded this is where everything of eternal significance gets birthed in the Kingdom.

Kasia Mysliwiec
FIRE School of Ministry Alumnus

A very moving story about a special relationship between two men of God! While some young leaders would seek to turn themselves into the image of their elders, this account reveals the ingredients of a healthy mentoring relationship: mutual admiration and respect, a deep love for one another, and a burning desire to glorify God rather than self. I highly recommend this book to everyone, especially to young people, as a model of what God seeks to accomplish in us through our spiritual elders.

Rev. Bob Honeysett
Founder and Director of Matthew 19:26 Ministries

Charles Simpson opens his soul to the reader and reveals the natural, unforced development of spiritual sonship. Through his unique story, we are privileged to participate in his relationship with David Wilkerson. I recommend this intriguing book to those who want to know more about "spiritual fathering" or are interested in the founder of Teen Challenge and Times Square Church.

David Harwood
Restoration Fellowship & Director of Love of God Project

This book gives us a delightful view into the life and ministry of David Wilkerson. Charles is a friend who lives and breathes the Gospel message. I'm grateful for the legacy of David Wilkerson and for such a unique perspective on one of God's generals in the faith. The desperate days we live in require the type of desperate faith and passion for God described in this book!

DR. BRIAN SIMMONS
The Passion Translation Project

My friend Charles Simpson experienced a dimension of David Wilkerson's amazing life that only a few had the honor to know. Once I began reading this manuscript, I couldn't put it down. Not only did I see into the heart of David Wilkerson and the keys to his successful ministry, but I also saw the profound effect he had on a spiritual son. What an inspiring book!

ROGER LEHMAN
Founder of City Streams Network & House of Glory

This book is powerful, exciting, easy to read, and wisdom-imparting! Like his spiritual father, David Wilkerson, Pastor Charles is a pastor to pastors, a man of integrity, motivated by the compassion of Jesus. A very enjoyable read that will definitely bring you closer to the Lord!

PETER KEMP
Pastor, Hope Chapel, Queens Foursquare Church

This is a great testimony of what God does to honor prayer and a man's commitment to follow Him through the leaders placed in his life. Pastor Charles reflects the importance of prayer, being obedient to the call of God upon one's life, and trusting the Lord for all things. This book will richly bless you!

VICTOR HARRIS
Director, Albany Teen Challenge

Within the pages of this book are the secrets of the spiritual success of my mentor and spiritual father, David Wilkerson. While he was not perfect, every fiber of his heart beat with a desire to please the Lord. I was invited by Brother Dave to sing regularly at Times Square Church and will forever cherish those times as the greatest moments in the ministry with which God has entrusted me. His words still echo in my spirit: "Mary Ann, always remember, it is not what you're doing for Christ that matters as much as what you are becoming for Christ!" This book will encourage you to impact the mission field to which the Lord has called you.

MARY ANN PELUSO
Worship Singer

Once I started reading this book, I couldn't put it down. I have great admiration for the life and ministry of David Wilkerson. Pastor Charles Simpson has captured it and has been captured by it. The mentorship, spiritual sonship, up-close-and-personal life experiences he had with David Wilkerson are evident in his own life and ministry. Pastor Charles's heart for the hurting, passion for prayer, and fatherly love are all reflections of walking in the footsteps of David Wilkerson. Charles Simpson serves as the Campus Pastor at Brooklyn Teen Challenge, and I was honored to minister alongside him. Without a doubt, the heart of David Wilkerson lives on at Brooklyn Teen Challenge!

REV. RUSSELL HODGINS
Senior Pastor of Fountain of Life Center
Burlington, New Jersey

I highly recommend Pastor Charles Simpson. He has a strong holiness message, but it is balanced with great love, mercy, and compassion. He is truly a man of prayer and he knows how to hear from God. He has been a vital part of our ministry in New York.

(The Late) DAVID WILKERSON
Teen Challenge, World Challenge, Times Square Church
and the author of *The Cross and the Switchblade*

WALKING IN THE FOOTSTEPS OF

DAVID
WILKERSON

WALKING IN THE FOOTSTEPS OF

DAVID WILKERSON

THE JOURNEY AND REFLECTIONS OF A SPIRITUAL SON

———————•◆•———————

CHARLES SIMPSON

DESTINY IMAGE® PUBLISHERS, INC.

P.O. Box 310, Shippensburg, PA 17257-0310

"Promoting Inspired Lives."

This book and all other Destiny Image and Destiny Image Fiction books are available at Christian bookstores and distributors worldwide.

Cover design by Eileen Rockwell
Interior design by Terry Clifton

For more information on foreign distributors, call 717-532-3040.
Or reach us on the Internet: www.destinyimage.com.

ISBN 13 TP: 978-0-7684-1750-0
ISBN 13 EBook: 978-0-7684-1751-7
ISBN LP: 978-0-7684-1753-1
ISBN HC: 978-0-7684-1752-4

For Worldwide Distribution, Printed in the U.S.A.
1 2 3 4 5 6 / 20 19 18

Dedicated to the love of my life, my dear wife, Lynn.

Contents

Foreword

As a seasoned leader who worked closely with Pastor David Wilkerson at Times Square Church, Charles Simpson invites us all to come behind the scenes with him to see what he saw and learn what he learned. From 1991 to 1995, I had the privilege of speaking at Times Square Church between forty and fifty times, often getting to fellowship with Pastor Dave before or after the service. Those were unforgettable times, and my esteem for him only increased as the years went on. I already knew Pastor Dave to be a real man of God, one of the great leaders of our generation. But the more time I spent with him, the more I was impressed with the depth of his spirituality—his prophetic insight, his wisdom, his love for Jesus, his hunger for the Spirit, his generosity, and his compassion.

Although he welcomed me warmly and treated me graciously, giving me carte blanche to preach from his pulpit, I never felt totally relaxed in his presence. I told some friends that hanging out with Pastor Dave was like fellowshipping with a razor blade! His eyes were so piercing you felt like he was looking right through you. And even though there was no condemnation in his speech, you wanted to be sure you didn't sit down with him having any unconfessed sin in your life. Somehow, you thought, he would know if you did. When

1

he would bring a prophetic warning from the pulpit, his heart broken in two and his spirit deeply grieved, everything in me exploded with affirmation. His burden was my burden too.

While ministering at Times Square Church, I met Charles Simpson, who was then serving as the pastor of prayer. And boy, can Charles pray! (Times Square Church was a praying church so you had to be a praying person to be appointed the pastor of prayer.) Charles also has a tremendously sincere love for the Lord that is not hardened by New York City and not stained by professional ministry. He has a humble servant's heart and an unfeigned love for Jesus and His people. Charles and I quickly became good friends.

Several years later, when my leadership team opened a branch of FIRE School of Ministry in Manhattan, we asked Charles to be one of the main teachers there, and he helped pastor our small student body. This brought us together even closer, and for good reason, our students fell in love with Charles and his wife, Lynn. Although we had to close our New York branch after a few years, I've continued to follow Charles's ministry, especially his writing ministry. When he told me about this book, I was thrilled. What better way to gain insight into the life of a giant of the faith like David Wilkerson than through the firsthand accounts of one of his spiritual sons? And what better way to learn practical ministry lessons—really, practical life lessons—than from the personal experiences of a devoted servant like Charles Simpson?

As I was preparing to write this foreword, I found a YouTube video of what was reported to be Pastor Dave's last recorded message, not long before he died in a tragic car accident at the age of eighty. As I watched that sermon (he had to teach sitting in a chair because of some health issues), I was stirred and challenged again, saying to myself, "We don't have anyone like him today." (At least, there is no one I know of personally who carries what he carried.) The good news is that through this book, you can sit at the feet of this departed man of God, hearing things that he never preached in public and learning lessons that he shared only with those who were close to him.

I'm so glad that Charles has shared his own story here, one that is deeply interwoven with the life of David Wilkerson. The pages that follow will surely bless and enrich you!

—DR. MICHAEL L. BROWN
Host of *The Line of Fire* Radio Broadcast

Introduction

Though you might have ten thousand instructors in Christ, yet you do not have many fathers... (1 Corinthians 4:15).

...walk in the steps of the faith which our father Abraham had (Romans 4:12).

I'VE BEEN TOLD THAT WE SHOULD NEVER FOLLOW A MAN, WE SHOULD follow only the Lord. Otherwise, we'll become disappointed or disillusioned. Perhaps. If anyone other than God becomes our main focus, or if we develop unrealistic expectations, of course we'll become disappointed. However, the Apostle Paul had some things to say along these lines. Quite often (while under divine inspiration, I might add), he instructed us to follow him:

Be followers of me... (1 Corinthians 4:16 KJV).

Follow my example, as I follow the example of Christ... (1 Corinthians 11:1 NIV).

Keep putting into practice all you learned and received from me—everything you heard from me and saw me doing. Then the God of peace will be with you (Philippians 4:9 NLT).

Abraham is another example of a man whose footsteps we are instructed to follow:

> ...walk in the steps of the faith which our father Abraham had... (Romans 4:12).

From the earliest days of my Christian walk in the 1970s until now, David Wilkerson's example has been profoundly influential. While working with him on staff at Times Square Church, I saw firsthand how passionate about and dedicated to the Lord he was, and I did my best to learn all I could from him. The lessons I received and our many conversations are more valuable to me than gold. What a wonderful pastor, evangelist, father, and prophet he was!

Aware that appreciation is only a few steps away from worship, I keep in mind that we all have "feet of clay."[1] If we follow even the best examples with a reckless abandon, we'll undoubtedly inherit their blind spots and their inevitable areas of weakness. Even so, how many "Davids" do you know (in any generation) who have slain more giants than David Wilkerson? Let me list some of these giants for you:

The giant problem of urban gang violence in the 1950s and 60s.

A skinny preacher from Pennsylvania had the audacity to believe that through him, God could save the likes of Nicky Cruz, the notorious leader of the Mau Maus gang in Brooklyn.

The giants of heroin, crack, alcohol, and other life-controlling addictions.

Teen Challenge, now with over 1,100 centers in 110 countries, is by far the most successful drug rehabilitation program in history. Just as King Saul's entire army shook in their boots over the thought of going against Goliath, the "experts" in the 1950s considered heroin addiction insurmountable.

***The giant need to lead many people to Christ during the Jesus
People and Charismatic movements.***

Traveling with the singing group Dallas Holm & Praise, David
Wilkerson conducted evangelistic services throughout the country,
helping to launch the Charismatic movement in Catholic and Epis-
copal churches. He led countless hippies and other young people to
the Lord.

***The giant need for a strong and consistent word from God to an
anemic American church.***

For decades, hundreds of thousands of believers eagerly antici-
pated the arrival of David Wilkerson's timely, powerful, convicting
newsletters in our mailboxes.

***The huge need for a Gospel witness in Times Square, the
crossroads of the world, which had become a cesspool of sin and
filth in the 1980s.***

Times Square Church, now over twenty-five years old, was
miraculously birthed through the faith and vision of Pastor Dave.
This congregation has stood as a beacon of truth and righteous-
ness for this city and for the Body of Christ worldwide. Truly, fruit
that remains.

The slaying of one of these five giants would probably qualify
someone to be listed in an updated "Faith Hall of Fame," found in
Hebrews chapter 11. For God to use one man to accomplish so much,
surely it's worthwhile to take a closer look at his unique life and
amazing walk of faith.

On many occasions, Pastor Dave told me I was like a son to
him, and he was certainly a spiritual father to me. However, with
privilege comes responsibility. Have I lived up to the responsibili-
ties of being one of his many spiritual sons? I hope so. Like Pastor
Dave, I came from a small town to the dangerous neighborhoods
of New York City. However, walking in the faith-filled steps of

Father Abraham doesn't mean that we all must live as tent dwelling patriarchs in the deserts of the Middle East! Following in David Wilkerson's footsteps refers more to *how* we live our Christian lives than to *what* we accomplish for the Lord. Even though we might not be called to build international ministries like Pastor Dave did, we all still have our God-appointed giants to conquer.

After Pastor Dave was suddenly promoted to glory in April 2011, I felt compelled to write down what I learned from this man of God before many of his edifying words spoken personally to me would begin to fade from my memory. I wrote almost non-stop for a number of weeks and then put this manuscript on the shelf for a few years. When I shared it with one of my Bible school students last year, he couldn't stop telling me how much it encouraged him. I asked one of David Wilkerson's relatives to read through it, and she felt that it was definitely worth sharing with others. So, I took it off the shelf and decided to have it published. One of the greatest lessons we can learn from Pastor Dave is the fact that God can take an ordinary person and teach him or her how to walk in extraordinary faith. As his brother Don once said, "David's life shows us that God can use anyone to save anyone." In other words, a country preacher armed with faith in God can reach hardened gang members who seem to be unredeemable. How can we also walk in that same type of faith? As I share my journey and how Pastor Dave deeply impacted my life, I'll endeavor to answer that important question.

My dad died when I was sixteen and he was sixty-one. When I wrote about Dad years later, some of my older siblings hardly recognized the gentle, mellow father I had come to know and love. Likewise, the six years I worked closely with David Wilkerson are only one slice of the whole pie. I daresay the David Wilkerson of the 1960s was a very different man than the one with whom I worked. Every chapter title is a quote from Pastor Dave. However, this book is not a full biography of his life but rather a journey through mine, emphasizing his constant and positive influence upon me.[2] May what I have written inspire you to rise up and become a conqueror of the giants in your personal life and in your generation!

1

"Every piece will still love you."

FROM DEEP WITHIN THE SANCTUARY, LOUD AND DESPERATE SCREAMS were heard: "Stop that man! He just stole a purse from one of the choir members! Stop him!" Mark and I were both standing at the front door of the church, the only way out. We could easily have prevented that guy from getting past us if we had had a few seconds to process what was happening. We should have at least tried to trip him as he flew past us. He tucked a large leather purse under his shirt like it was a football and ran down the street, darting around people and poles and cars. He crossed Seventh Avenue and disappeared down the subway steps. Mark and I looked at each other, nodded in agreement, and took off after him.

After all, we were in charge of security in the new church. It had been going for only a few months, but already hundreds of people were attending. How was that possible? David Wilkerson announced Times Square Church's opening through his mailing list many months before starting in Town Hall. He rented those facilities for Sunday morning and Tuesday evening services. A few weeks after a very successful launch, the church outgrew that space and moved into the Nederlander Theatre on 41st Street, right in the middle of busy Manhattan. The services were packed, dynamic, and filled with spiritually hungry people from across the Tri-State region.

David Wilkerson, the author of the best-selling book (and movie) *The Cross and the Switchblade,* heard from God that he was to raise up a church in Times Square of all places! Surely God had not written off New York City, as many people in the Body of Christ had been feeling for the past few years. The mass exodus to the suburbs had officially ended. The Lord still had great plans for this city! The enthusiasm and expectations were so high that everyone involved was extremely excited, including me and Mark. We were both in our twenties and felt so blessed to be on staff. Along with Wally and Alex, we actually lived in the theater, and our duties were to maintain the facilities and handle security issues. Sometimes we found homeless people hiding in the bathroom stalls or in the closets after church services were over. A few times, we discovered the door to the roof opened, apparently because someone was intending to come back in the middle of the night to take whatever they could carry out.

We never actually had anyone come into the building in broad daylight and steal anything, not until the purse snatcher. The female choir members left their purses on the front row seats when they went up to the theater's stage to rehearse. The shady character walked right into the church and slowly made his way down the aisle. (Everyone must have assumed he came for an audition.) All the women's purses were in plain sight on the front row, right where they could keep an eye on them. That guy took the first purse he came to and took off like a late freight train. Mark and I noticed as we came to the top of the subway steps that he didn't anticipate anyone following him. There he was, on the bottom step, casually rummaging through the large purse as though it was his! He saw us coming and darted across the subway station, heading toward another stairway exit. We somehow reached that exit first and cornered him against a wall. I grabbed the purse from his trembling hands. (He must have been a drug addict.) Then I declared in my most authoritative voice,

"How dare you walk into a church and steal a purse...from a choir member!" I looked up the steps in the direction of the church, realizing it actually looked more like a theater than a house of worship.

When my eyes glanced back upon our little criminal, I saw his face grimacing as though he was exerting all his strength. Before I realized what was happening, he pulled out a long, razor-sharp screwdriver and plunged it toward my stomach. A second before it reached its target, Mark's hand came pounding down on his wrist, and the screwdriver fell to the ground. The addict reached down for it but suddenly decided against that course of action. He lifted himself up, took one last defiant look at us, and ran up the steps and back into the hustle and bustle of the city streets, never to be seen by us again.

Mark and I just stared at each other, soaking in all that had happened in the past three and a half minutes. He picked up the weapon and almost touched the tip of that screwdriver, but he decided against it because of its sharpened, razor-thin point.

"Thank you so much, Mark!" I exclaimed.

"Thank God, Charles. Thank God."

We soon noticed that the lady whose purse was stolen (and recovered) was nervously waiting in front of the church. On our way back, Mark jokingly repeated my remarks: "How dare you walk into a church and steal a purse from a choir member! Boy, Charles, you sure convicted him!" We broke out into hearty laughter, both because it was quite silly of me and because we were so relieved that things turned out OK.

As we approached the theater, Mark read aloud from a poster taped on the inside of one of its advertising windows: "Come hear David Wilkerson, the author of *The Cross and the Switchblade*." Mark then held up the screwdriver and joked, "Hey Charles, maybe one day you'll write a book called *The Cross and the Screwdriver*!" Again, another round of laughter as we entered the sanctuary and secured the doors behind us. For years after this incident, Mark would occasionally ask when I was going to write my book *The Cross and the Screwdriver*. I passed it off as a foolish notion. But for the next six years, I did my best to soak in all I could from Pastor Dave, who was such a great example of a man of God to all who received from him, either through his sermons or newsletters (regularly sent out to over a million homes) or by working alongside him. In the churches and Bible schools that I've pastored and taught in since, people have been blessed when I've shared bits and pieces of what I experienced and learned directly from him. Many times have I heard these words: "I just love it when you share your stories about David Wilkerson!" I will do my best to share everything exactly as it occurred, starting in Tennessee, thirty-nine years ago.

———————◆———————

Cleveland, Tennessee, is where the Church of God was birthed and where David Wilkerson's grandfather was from. This was where I experienced a spiritual rebirth as a teenager in 1978. It was such a peaceful little town, located about thirty miles northeast of Chattanooga. We moved there from Waverly, Tennessee, in the middle of my junior year of high school, right after Dad's funeral. One day I went to an art exhibit in the Cleveland mall. I was standing in front of a huge nine-foot by nine-foot painting of a dried-out dandelion flower that was ready to be plucked and blown away by the wind. I was still deeply grieving, still in shock over the passing of my father. At the suggestion of my concerned mom, I went to try to get my mind off my constant grief and on other things.

A tall man quietly walked over to the same painting and started thinking out loud: "Isn't it amazing," he began, as he kept his eyes glued to the painting, "with all those seeds, only one-fourth of them will find good soil. One-fourth will be trodden down and eaten by birds. Some will spring up on rocky soil, and others will be choked by weeds. Only a portion of these many seeds will actually produce anything." I had been reading the New Testament constantly, so I knew he was referring to Jesus's parable of the sower. I almost proudly replied, "I know, the parable of the sower...Matthew chapter 13." He turned to me and said, "It doesn't matter how many Scriptures you know. You can know the entire Bible and still not know God and die without Christ and go to hell."

"Oh my gosh," I thought to myself, "how does this guy know I spend my spare time reading the Bible? He must be some sort of prophet, like Jeremiah or Daniel. He sure has my attention!" For the next few minutes, I stood there completely mesmerized as this guy spoke about the pain of losing loved ones, the torture of adjusting to too many new things at one time, and the blessings in becoming a born-again Christian. As he continued speaking about God, Heaven, and eternity, I could somehow feel the authenticity of his words. Pure authenticity is hard to describe if you've never heard it before; it's like describing the color blue to a person born blind.

"Everything you see, everything will one day burn up, but our souls are eternal. We will live eternally with or without God...with Christ or without Christ." For the first time in my life, I felt the presence of God. I wanted to fall on my knees right there in front of Radio Shack and say, "How do I become born again?" Instead, I gave in to my fears and told this prophet guy, "See ya," and I rudely and quickly walked away.

A few months later, our paths crossed again! This time he asked assertively, "Would you like to come to my church next Sunday morning?" This twenty-something-year-old guy named Charles Thompson sure was kind. But as far as I could remember, I had never in my life gone to a church service or even entered a church building. As I finally answered, my voice got fainter and slower until I was nearly whispering. The words were that painful. "I'm still in high school, and my mom doesn't drive, and my dad died, and...I don't know." As a self-absorbed, hurting teenager who wasn't sure about Christianity, I imagined he was thinking, "What a loser" and that he'd just walk away. Instead, he put his right hand on my shoulder and replied compassionately, "Don't worry, man. I'll pick you up," speaking with a cheerfulness that was foreign to my world.

Every Sunday he did what he said he would do: he took me with him in his old backfiring Pinto to Keith Street Church of God of Prophecy. Our trips back and forth were somewhat awkward. I didn't know what to say. I secretly wondered why he wanted to be friends with a shy, hurting kid who wasn't even sure if God existed. "Maybe it's all a myth," I'd often say to myself, parroting my older siblings' opinions. Besides, it all seemed too good to be true, like a well-written fairy tale—delightful to hear, but not grounded in real life. The love expressed in the Bible seemed too unreal to me, too disconnected from real life, too much for my heart to believe...until Testimony Sunday.

Testimony Sunday was a quarterly occasion at the church. On that particular day, the preacher shared for only a few minutes, and then he opened the floor for whoever wanted to testify. Charles Thompson was the second one to stand, and he waited for the usher to hand him the microphone before beginning. He said, "God's been dealing with me lately about walking in love. I witnessed to this teen-ager a few months ago." He paused and looked down at me, sitting beside him. "I offered to give him a ride to church. He accepted, and I've been doing it ever since. I never told him that I live on the other end of Bradley County and that I have to get up earlier on Sunday mornings now than I ever imagined I would...or could."

Everyone seemed to laugh and clap their hands—everyone except me. I was thinking, "Where's he going with this?" He contin-ued, "But how could I tell him that God so loved the world that He sent His Son all the way from Heaven to earth to die for us, and that that same God now lives in my heart, and then tell him that he lives too far for me to pick him up?" He looked down at me again with an expression that said, "I hope this hasn't embarrassed you." I looked up and saw the compassion of Christ looking down at me through him, and I saw God's love in him. I suddenly knew that it was all real and true and that this man was reaching out to me because Jesus Christ lives in him. Jesus Christ, the resurrected Son of the living God, was actually reaching out to me through him!

The following day, as soon as I had a chance to be alone, I repented of my sins and asked Jesus to be the Lord of my life. The immediate and overwhelming peace that flooded my soul assured me that my prayer had been answered! The first one to call was my new friend, Charles Thompson. He was thrilled and immediately asked if I would like to spend next Sunday morning in church with him, and the rest of the day as well. I knew Mom wouldn't mind so I accepted his offer. Charles Thompson was excited about my spending an afternoon with him and "the guys." For weeks, he'd been sharing with me about the Christian ministry he was in. Previously, he had given me some literature regarding the dramatic conversion of the Charismatic director of Reality of Life Ministries, Mike, a man who had been the leader of a gang in the South Bronx called the Young Aces in the 1960s.

One humid New York City summer, the police were hot on Mike's trail and determined to put him behind bars for good. He accepted an invitation from relatives to visit them in Cleveland, Tennessee. While there, he encountered the resurrected Lord at a Church of God camp meeting. He was immediately and completely delivered from his heroin addiction. The first thing Mike did was to return to the city and report to his parole officer. He had broken parole by leaving the state without permission. The dumbfounded officer demanded a urine sample, which came back negative. Soon afterward, a blood test provided remarkable evidence of Mike's conversion and deliverance. His blood showed no evidence of any drug use ever and was actually as pure as a newborn baby's. The parole officer was deeply touched by Mike's change of heart and the physical manifestation that accompanied his spiritual new birth.

The parole officer wasn't the only one impacted by Mike's conversion. Within the period of about a month, Mike was able to lead over half of his former gang members to a salvation experience. The other half of those angry Young Aces collected enough money among themselves to hire a professional hitman to kill their former leader. When a hitman named Eddie knocked on Mike's South Bronx apartment door, he had a loaded and cocked .357 Magnum revolver hidden in his leather jacket.

The door opened wide, and Eddie asked him, "Are you Mike?"

"Yes, I am," Mike responded with a smile. "And you, you have been mad at God ever since your father died when you were six years old."

"What? Wait a minute," Eddie said, shaking his head as if needing to awaken from a nightmare. "How do you know this about me?" he demanded.

Mike took a step closer and said, "When I opened the door, I saw inside of you the broken heart of a six-year-old boy. I saw you standing near a casket as someone told you, 'God took him.' It wasn't God. It was alcohol, cirrhosis of the liver. It was the devil who took him, the same stinking devil who's been lying to you your whole life."

Eddie stepped a few feet back, his eyes filled with shock and tears. He slowly pulled out his loaded gun and lowered it as he also lowered his eyes and head. "I'm a good-for-nothin' hitman. I came to blow your brains out tonight for a measly five hundred bucks. If God really showed you this, does this mean that He cares...about me? I mean...could He forgive *me?*" Mike led him in the sinner's prayer that evening and soon made him a part of his ministry. They ministered together in various churches and street outreaches throughout the metropolitan area. As the ministry grew, many of the gang members who got saved didn't have homes to go back to. Mike decided to follow the examples of two of his heroes, David Wilkerson and Keith Green. Both had residential programs for young believers with life-controlling problems. Teen Challenge and Last Days Ministries became role models for Reality of Life Ministries.

Mike's testimony was broadcast throughout the world on the radio drama *UNSHACKLED!* from Pacific Garden Mission in Chicago. Enough funds came in to purchase a farm near Cleveland, Tennessee. In the summer, he would still evangelize on the streets of the Big Apple. For those who got saved and had nowhere to go, he'd bring them home with him to Tennessee. Throughout the winter months, these new believers received constant discipleship and nurturing twenty-four hours a day, seven days a week. Mike, his sweet wife Naomi, and their two little boys were happy to share their home and hearts with these young men. One of those converts was none other than Charles Thompson, the man who led me to Christ.

Charles and I were driving down the highway, heading toward the farmhouse. "I know you've met some of the guys in church already. It's a good time for you to come and meet the rest of us. Mike travels a lot, but he's in town this weekend. We're going to watch a movie this afternoon called *The Cross and the Switchblade.* David Wilkerson is one of our heroes, and Mike wants everyone to be familiar with his ministry and Nicky Cruz's testimony." As I walked into a huge living room, I realized why Charles waited until I accepted Christ before bringing me there. The room was filled with ex-heroin addicts, ex-gang members, ex-speed freaks, and ex-criminals. They were loud, boisterous, obnoxious, and totally New Yorkish. Besides Charles Thompson and Kenny, I was the only other white guy in the group. That didn't bother them or me because these guys were now my brothers.

"Hey brothers! Here's my friend, Charles Simpson! He accepted the Lord this past week. Isn't that great?" They all bombarded me with high fives and bear hugs. As we sat down, munched on fresh popcorn, and watched the movie, at least five times one of the guys spilled his popcorn, jumping up in excitement over familiar movie scenes portrayed on the television screen. *The Cross and the*

Switchblade tells the amazing story of a young pastor of a small-town American church who embarked on a mission to help the members of troubled street gangs in New York City. In the late 1950s, a gang of teenagers viciously killed a polio-stricken, fifteen-year-old boy named Michael Farmer. Through prayer and reading about that incident in *LIFE Magazine*, David Wilkerson felt that God's will for him was to travel from rural Pennsylvania to the rough streets of New York City. One of the highlights of the movie was when a notorious gang leader seriously threatened him. A strange and heavy silence fell on all of us as we watched Nicky Cruz threaten the skinny country preacher.

"You come near me, and I'll kill you!"

David Wilkerson replied, "Yeah, you could do that. You could cut me up into a thousand pieces and lay them in the street, and every piece will still love you."

Tears welled up in my eyes as I saw the love of Christ displayed on the screen in front of me—the same unselfish love I saw in Charles Thompson. "Every piece will still love you." Wow! Maybe one day, with God's help, I'll be able to love like that. Maybe, just maybe, if God could so use a young preacher from Pennsylvania, He could also use my life to bring others into His Kingdom. After the movie, I stayed glued to the couch as everyone else went off to various appointments or work assignments. Eventually, I slid off the couch and onto my knees and began to cry as an overwhelming feeling came over me. The Lord was speaking to my trembling heart: "If you let Me fill you with the same type of love you saw in David Wilkerson, I will also send you to the broken and the hurting."

I quickly became friends with all those precious guys and hung out with them every Sunday afternoon and evening. They soon invited me to travel with them on Wednesday evenings. They visited various churches in the region to give their testimonies. Often they would show a slide presentation of the needs of New York City: a picture of a homeless man slouched over in a subway car, a dear lady sleeping on the streets in a measly cardboard box, a girl with scary dark rings under her eyes showing the photographer the many needle marks on her skeletal arms. Each time I saw those pictures, a burden deep in my heart got a little stronger. I knew God was using those images to strengthen a call to the broken and hurting, to the mission field of lost souls, to the asphalt jungles of New York City.

By the time I graduated high school, I totally agreed with Keith Green, the director of Last Days Ministries, who wrote: "I don't believe that God wants every Christian to go to college just because, 'Well, everyone goes to college now, unless they're too dumb!' You shouldn't go to college unless God has definitely called you to go. Just like everything else in our Christian lives, He's the Master, we're the servants. He's the General, we're the soldiers. If you're really a Christian, you're at the beck and command of the King. If you're not at His command, then you're really not a Christian."[3]

Boy, was my unsaved family upset! I made As in high school and could have gone to any college I wanted. Telling them it wasn't up to me but up to Jesus to decide what my next steps would be sounded ludicrous to them. Even more ridiculous was accepting a full-time, live-in position at the ministry farmhouse as a counselor/intern for the salary of just room and board! I would have paid to have the privilege of being part of a ministry that daily saw lives transformed right before our very eyes.

2

"Because they were sold out to God, they were given supernatural courage!"

As SPRINGTIME APPROACHED, STAFF MEMBERS WERE HOPING AND expecting Mike to choose them as his traveling and preaching companion for his upcoming evangelistic outreaches in New York City. Mike's father, Miguel, who lived in the South Bronx, came for visits to the farmhouse because Mike didn't always bring his wife and kids with him on his journeys to the Big Apple. Miguel was a frail but very friendly man. I liked him immediately, and we hit it off right away. But I couldn't understand how Miguel could witness a transformation in his son and not also enthusiastically follow the Lord. He would joke, "I know Jesus could deliver me from this," as he'd hold up a whiskey bottle wrapped in a brown paper bag. "But I don't want to be delivered!" No wonder Mike wasn't overjoyed when his father came to stay.

One morning during Miguel's visit, I woke up to a quiet, empty house. It seemed that everyone had places to go and things to do that day. On the large dining room table, propped up by the centerpiece so I wouldn't miss it, was a yellow writing tablet with this note, written with a black magic marker:

> Charles, after you feed the animals, could you please change the starter in the Pinto? The new one is on the freezer, along with the tools you'll need. Thanks, and we'll all be back this evening. Mike.

I guessed Miguel wanted to go sightseeing. "Man," I thought to myself, "I don't know how to change a starter!" I looked out the window and noticed that someone had placed a mechanic's blanket on the concrete driveway under the Pinto for me. It couldn't be too hard. I decided to attempt the repairs before feeding myself or any of the farm animals. If I couldn't do it, I'd have the rest of the day to find someone who could. I found the new starter and the tools, crawled under the car, and got to work. The screws on the old starter were very hard to loosen. For a while, I wasn't sure if I could even get them all off. I was relieved when the last one finally loosened. As I began unscrewing it, it didn't dawn on me that gravity was about to kick in. Down it suddenly fell, right onto the concrete, smashing one of my fingers in the process. "Well, praise the Lord anyway," I said out loud as I immediately began examining the cut. "Thank You, Jesus, that it's not too deep." I grabbed a nearby rag, ripped off a few inches, tied it around my throbbing, bloody finger and completed the job. (It would only leave a small scar on my finger.)

As I walked into the house to wash up, I was startled to see Miguel pouring himself a cup of coffee. I said to him, "I thought you went out with Mike today."

"I was going to," Miguel said as he sipped his coffee and stared at me from behind his cup as though he'd never seen a white boy from Tennessee before. "At the last minute I decided to stay here." When Miguel said goodbye to me a few days later, I never imagined I'd see him again soon.

About a month later, my roommate Pete and I were in our room in the farmhouse, enjoying our day off together. Pete was listening to a cassette tape of a man preaching about Aaron and the golden calf he made for Israel to worship. Suddenly, the preacher compared the episode of Moses coming off the mountain and angrily throwing down the Ten Commandment tablets to the anger God feels over His lukewarm church in America. As the sermon continued, the preacher's voice got stronger and louder until he was yelling. But it was inspired yelling, like how a father would yell to his toddler who's about to run out into heavy traffic. The preacher said, "Within that entire multitude of people who came out of Egypt with Moses, only two men followed the Lord with all their hearts—Joshua and Caleb. Because they were sold out to God, they were given supernatural courage!"

"That guy's anointed!" I exclaimed. "Who is that, Pete?"

"You don't know? That's David Wilkerson."

"David Wilkerson! The same guy in the movie?"

"Nooo. The guy in the movie was Pat Boone. He's a Christian actor who played David Wilkerson. This is the real David Wilkerson!"

Angel then yelled up the staircase from the first floor. "Mike's calling a ministry meeting in the living room right now."

"Oh boy," Pete exclaimed as we began to walk down the steps together. "He's gonna announce who's going with him to New York this summer. It has to be my turn this year! Charles Thompson went last year, and Angel the year before. It's my time, man!"

Mike had a weird look on his face. Then what came out of his mouth was even weirder. "Umm...I gotta leave for New York earlier than usual this year. Papi's really sick in the hospital. I got this letter from him today. Gotta go tomorrow. Don't know when I'll return. Let's pray."

"Wait," Angel interrupted. "Who's going with you?"

"Charles Simpson." Startled grunts and groans filled the room.

"WHAT!" Pete loudly protested, expressing what everyone else was thinking. "Mike, are you crazy? He's just an intern! Besides, it's my turn to go. Why in the world would you pick him over me?" Pete looked over at me, and if looks could kill, I would have dropped dead right then and there. I was glad he didn't carry weapons anymore!

"Pedro, ¡cállate!" Mike said in an authoritative tone that I think meant "shut up and listen!" "I didn't pick him over you. Papi did. Listen to this letter." He unfolded it and read it aloud: "Dear son, I hate this hospital and I hate this food. Doctors aren't giving me long to live. If you wanna see me again, come now. And bring Charles Simpson with you. There's something inside that young man I've never seen before. He actually didn't curse when the starter fell on his finger. He even thanked God that it didn't cut him too badly. Please bring him with you. Love, Papi."

I looked down at the tiny scar on my finger, as everyone stared at me in shock. I added the details of what happened that morning, noting that I didn't even know Miguel was around. How ironic that the little bit of self-control I exhibited that day revealed Christ to someone who had already seen so many lives transformed. I might not run across hardened gang members like Nicky Cruz in New York City, but maybe, just maybe, if I went with Mike, I'd be able to lead dear Miguel to the Lord before he entered eternity.

For the first time in my life, I flew on an airplane—from Chattanooga to New York City. My mission was to reach Miguel before he passed away and to assist Mike with his evangelistic campaigns. I was nineteen years old, and it was a very cold March in 1980. I had been a Christian for only two years, and I was as nervous as I was excited about visiting New York City for a few months, or maybe longer. When we arrived at LaGuardia Airport, the place was packed. "I've never seen so many people in one place before," I kept mumbling to Mike as I hustled to keep up with him.

He turned back toward me and said impatiently, "You haven't seen anything yet. And close that gaping mouth of yours. You look like a gullible tourist." I felt more like a tourist than an assistant to a world-famous evangelist. Well, maybe not world famous yet. Mike looked worried, and I knew he was already having second thoughts about bringing me with him. We went straight from the airport to St. Barnabas Hospital. Mike and I both fervently prayed for his dad. He was too sedated to talk (or at least he pretended to be), so we made our way over to Miguel's apartment in the South Bronx via a wild taxi ride. The taxi cabs were like a bunch of yellow demons, disregarding every traffic law. Amazing! By the time we arrived, the sun had gone down. At the end of a dingy hallway, we found Miguel's apartment door. It had four locks on it. Four! One of them was called a police lock. It consisted of a steel pole attached to the floor and the inside of the door. "Wow!" I thought to myself. "We never lock any of our doors in Tennessee." (If I had kept expressing out loud how weird this place was to me, Mike would surely have sent me home on the first flight out the next day.)

Mike settled into bed in Miguel's room, and I got into a sleeping bag on the living room floor. The sofa was nothing more than a small loveseat; it was much too small for me. As I was about to doze off, I heard a rattling noise by my feet. "Oh no," I said to myself. "Sounds like a rattlesnake! Does Miguel have a pet snake? Do people in this city actually keep them as pets? There it goes again. It's definitely coming from behind that chair." But as quickly as it started, it suddenly stopped. I finally was about to escape into dreamland when the snake started up again. This time it was louder and longer. About fifteen terrifying minutes later, it stopped. I realized the whole apartment was quite warm. "Aha! That's not a snake." I walked over to the lamp beside the chair and bravely turned on the light. I saw what the head of my snake really was—an old, rusty cap to a radiator connected to a steam boiler in the basement. I had come so close to running into Mike's room, hysterically screaming,

"There's a rattlesnake in here!" He would have sent me back to Tennessee for sure.

As morning came, I awoke to a new world. People have often asked me what it was like going from a small town in Tennessee to the South Bronx. Was it like traveling to China? No, more like traveling to a new planet. I laid in my sleeping bag for a few minutes, realizing that everything was...different. It was the smallest apartment I'd ever been in. The "rattlesnake" heating system was definitely new to me. The smell of Bustelo coffee filled the air as Mike sang in a foreign language. We soon made our way out to the Hub, a busy section of the South Bronx. Three major streets intersected there. I realized that everything was foreign to me: the way people dressed, what they ate, and how they talked and even walked! Also, their pace of life, the smells, the sights, the sounds; the list went on and on.

The next day, Mike needed to go to Grand Central Station to get a train to Connecticut to visit a sponsor. He decided to take me with him to the Metro North train, and then I'd return to Miguel's apartment on my own. I would just have to retrace my steps. As we arrived at Grand Central Station, my jaw opened really wide once again. Underneath the ground there were various types of small grocery stores, retail stores, restaurants, and all kinds of places. There was a bank and a shoe store, and even a barbershop! It dawned on me: we were actually in an underground city!

I grabbed Mike's arm, and he stopped walking for a moment. I quickly whispered into his ear, "Mike, is this where the Mafia is located?"

"What do you mean? The Mafia's all over this city."

"No, Mike. I mean, is this their headquarters?"

"What?" He looked at me quizzically and resumed his brisk walk through the maze of Grand Central Station.

"Isn't this the underground world? I mean, isn't the Mafia in the underground?"

Mike gazed at me with a puzzled look and then cracked a smile and said, "That's a good joke, Charles. The underground world! You are joking, right? Please tell me you're joking." I wasn't joking, but I guess I should have been. My naiveté was just beginning to show itself.

A few days later, I met some tenants in the building: a cool guy named Bobby and his girlfriend, Madelyn Cohen. One of the screws holding my glasses together fell off as Mike and I were walking somewhere in Manhattan. He said, "There's an eyeglass store on this block. Let's stop and get that fixed right away."

When I noticed the name on the door, I got really excited. Cohen's Fashion Optical. As the clerk began working on my glasses, I asked if Mr. Cohen was around. The clerk looked up at me as if I had escaped from a mental hospital.

"What?" he rudely asked.

Mike quickly intervened, telling the guy that I was a tourist. With a very thick southern accent, I slowly continued, "But ain't this Cohen's Optical? I was just gonna ask Mr. Cohen if he knew Madelyn."

The bored clerk decided to play around with me, asking, "And who is Madelyn?"

"Madelyn Cohen lives in the Bronx, in the same apartment building as Mike's father. Y'all don't know Madelyn?"

The clerk and a few other co workers who joined the unusual conversation broke out in seemingly endless laughter. Afterward, a lady who must have been the manager of Cohen's Optical said to me, "Cohen's Fashion Optical was founded by Jack Cohen in 1926. We now have quite a few stores in several states. There are thousands of Cohens in New York City. The chances of Jack ever having met Madelyn are about a trillion to one." They began hysterically laughling again as Mike pushed me out the front door. I was in a different world than down south. If there were an eyeglass place in Cleveland, Tennessee, with the same last name of a neighbor, the chances of their being related are at least two to one. I was unable to explain that to Mike.

One evening, Mike went somewhere on his own. I decided to go back up to the rooftop of his father's apartment building. Mike had shown me previously how to unlock the roof door. We had spent time looking over "the hood" (short for neighborhood). I wanted to venture out into the dark city at night and explore that strange world, but Mike said it was too dangerous. Even two of us walking together at night would be too risky. On that isolated roof, I felt safe. I could see the post office where the notorious killer Son of Sam had worked. A few blocks away was Lincoln Hospital. I listened to the ambulance sirens as they approached one of the busiest emergency rooms in the country. Then I heard a police siren down the block. It started to die down, drowned out by a fire engine a few blocks away. Then another ambulance, a police siren a mile away, another fire truck nearby. For the next hour, I stood there startled that the sirens never stopped. What kind of place was this? It was said that the Bronx was burning, and I believed it. The slum landlords were having their own buildings burned down so they could collect the insurance money and get out of there. Fear suddenly gripped my heart, and I wondered if I'd ever get out of that surreal asphalt jungle alive. I recalled and recited aloud to myself the words I had heard from an anointed sermon: "Because they were sold out to God, they were given supernatural courage!" "Oh Lord," I fervently prayed, "I surrender my entire life to You."

Mike's dad took a turn for the better and was grateful to be back home in his little apartment. One rainy Sunday before going out for a full day of preaching engagements, Mike asked me to stay home and keep his dad company. Miguel and I decided to watch *West Side Story* on his small black-and-white television. The movie ripped my heart to pieces. It put names and faces on all the New Yorkers for whom I had been praying since I first saw Reality of Life Ministry's slide presentation in Tennessee. Who wouldn't feel for Tony and Maria? Their unsuccessful attempts to build a happy life together in the midst of the gang culture in the Big Apple were so heartbreaking. No wonder *West Side Story* won more Academy Awards than any other musical film in history. I tried hiding my tears from Miguel, but he was crying harder than me. It was the hundredth time he'd seen it, and only my first. He took a few tissues and then handed me the box. After it was over, he quickly turned the channel to some sporting event. Clearing his nose, he seemed to immediately forget all about the movie. Not me. I would never be the same.

I decided to fast and pray the next day, interceding for all the real-life Tonys and Marias I saw while Mike and I prayer-walked the streets of the Bronx and Spanish Harlem. I cried a lot that day. I wept over the lost, cried for Miguel, and also wept with gratitude that I was not a lost soul in that wicked city. That evening, Mike and I were invited to a Spanish pastor's apartment. We were to discuss rearranging his calendar to accommodate Mike's change of schedule. When we arrived, we found his living room filled with members of his church. They were the sweetest New Yorkers I'd ever met. We joined them in exuberant singing as they alternated between Spanish and English songs. After a long time of singing, the pastor jumped to his feet and asked if anyone wanted to testify. A lady next to me, with her hair in an extremely tight bun, stood up and shared in very broken English. She was grateful that her "Niño" in prison wrote her, saying he finally accepted the Lord. When she sat down, I stood up suddenly and shared how grateful I was that the Lord saved me. I hoped and prayed and believed that God would use me to win souls for His Kingdom. The words and the tears rolled out of me like a river. I could have stopped them, but I knew the anointing of the

Holy Spirit was upon me, so I continued speaking for quite a while. It wasn't until I sat down that I realized many others were weeping and praying. Some had even sunk out of their seats onto their knees. I turned to Mike and whispered, "I hope I didn't go too long."

He smiled affectionately, slapped my knee, and simply said, "No, you didn't."

At the end of the meeting, the pastor made a beeline right to me. I was thinking, "Oh no! Maybe I did testify too long and he's gonna rebuke me as only a New Yorker can."

Instead, he extended his hand and gave me a vigorous handshake. He said, "Young man, I have to go out of town next weekend, and I'd love for you to preach for me in my church while I'm gone."

In shock, I looked over at Mike, and he was smiling real big. He was nodding his head up and down a number of times. It finally registered in my frozen brain. "Uh, sure, Pastor. I'd be honored." Maybe I should have said, "You've got to be kidding! Surely you have the wrong guy. I've never preached a sermon in my life." I frantically began preparing one in my head, right at that moment. I thought about it on the ride home. I spent every spare minute the following week either working on the message, praying about it, or worrying about it.

Before I knew it, I was in his small church, being introduced to the congregation by one of the deacons. I preached my heart out. I preached all my sermon points, threw in everything I knew about Christ, looked down at my watch and was horrified to see that I'd gone only eighteen minutes! I kind of started over from the top and changed a few phrases so people wouldn't think I was being redundant. I looked down again and noticed I'd gone only five more minutes, a grand total of twenty-three minutes—way too short for a Pentecostal service. I paused and bowed my head and silently prayed, "Lord, what should I do now?"

The sweet Holy Spirit said to my trembling but listening heart, "Give an altar call for those who would like to get saved today." I was about to argue with those promptings because the smiles of encouragement on all the people's faces were a pretty good indication that those folks were already saved—and probably had been for a lot longer than me! I simply obeyed. I said that Jesus was there at the altar, ready to forgive and give a new life to anyone who would repent and call upon Him. Then I noticed a young man standing at the entrance of the front door, listening intently to my every word. He slowly made his way down the aisle. Gasps of "Thank You, Jesus" and "Hallelujah" could be heard from the stunned congregation. The young man, apparently a local gang member, came to the altar, fell to his knees, and began crying like a little toddler. Three deacons and I walked over to him as the pianist played some soft background music. The young man looked up at me with tears and snot running down his face and said, "What do I do now, Preacher?"

I didn't plan on this happening so I shrugged my shoulders and said, "I don't know." I had been so focused on planning the sermon, I didn't even think about the altar call. But, thank God, the deacons knew what to do, and they led him in the sinner's prayer as I went and sat down with Mike on the front row. The whole church was thrilled beyond measure, but none more than I. Except perhaps the young man who accepted Jesus that day! "Lord," I quietly whispered as we sang a song of rejoicing to conclude the meeting, "this is what I want to do with my life."

One evening, while visiting an old friend of Mike's, I was sitting on a large windowsill with a panoramic view of most of the South Bronx and parts of Manhattan. Everyone else was in the kitchen. I was alone in the living room—a rather large one for the Bronx. I was somewhere between daydreaming and praying when all of a sudden I had a vision of my last moments on this earth. I began soaring through the clouds into Heaven. I heard a voice say, "Look down." I thought about Lot's wife who turned into a pillar of salt when she looked back, so I didn't look down. A gentle inner voice said, "I want you to look back for just a moment to see from where you will leave this world." I looked down and saw New York City below me, quickly fading out of sight. I knew the gentle voice was the Lord's, and He was saying, "This is your new home, Charles. This is your mission field." Instantly, I knew that my visit to this city was more than just a temporary stay.

Mike came into the room and told me that Miguel had just prayed with him over the phone for the first time ever and had accepted Jesus as his Savior.

"Wonderful!" I joyfully exclaimed.

"I hope he meant it," Mike slowly commented with urban pessimism.

When I arrived back home, Miguel was sitting at the kitchen table with a strange snicker on his face and a brown paper bag in his hands with that hidden bottle inside. I grabbed it out of his hands and said, "Didn't the doctor tell you one more bottle could be the death of you?"

"Well, why don't you just pour it out into the bathroom sink for me then!" he yelled back as I stomped out of the room with it. I marched to the bathroom, and as I poured the junk down the drain, I noticed it smelled a lot more like Coca-Cola than alcohol. I looked inside the crumpled bag, and sure enough, it was a sixteen-ounce bottle of Pepsi! "You owe me a Pepsi," Miguel laughed, "and an apology."

"I'm sorry," I humbly and quickly replied.

"I know you care deeply about me, Charles. And I know that God cares. I believe in Christ. I really do. But remember, things are not always the way they seem."

"Because they were sold out to God, they were given supernatural courage!"

Those were the last words I heard him say. When Mike and I returned the following evening, we found him lying unconscious on the living room floor. The paramedics said it looked like he died of a massive heart attack a few hours before they arrived. Mike didn't sleep much for the next few days. He was busy making arrangements and calling Puerto Rico and other places, trying to track down relatives. He didn't eat much, either. I was concerned that the death of his father had totally broken his heart. At the dreary funeral, he was coughing his head off because a bad cold had set in. For days afterward, he would lie on his dad's bed, staring at the walls, coughing. He wouldn't eat, and he wouldn't go to the doctor. He wouldn't answer the phone. When I answered it for him, he wouldn't talk to anyone. I repeated to him over and over the last conversation I had with Miguel. I tried to convince Mike that his dad really did believe in the Lord at the end. Even that didn't seem to help.

With Mike lying in bed all day, all I could do was sit in the living room and pray. The more I prayed, the more it dawned on me that Mike was in severe danger. I called the guys in Tennessee. Pete answered and listened carefully to me. He then said, "Charles, the enemy is trying to take Mike out. Such a creep, kicking him while he's down."

"What should I do, Pete? Should I call an ambulance?"

"An ambulance? Is he that sick?"

"Pete, he's as pale as the bedroom walls, hasn't eaten in days, and won't take any medicine. I don't think he wants to get better. I don't think he wants to live anymore."

"You'd better call an ambulance, Charles. But before you do, pray for him."

"Pete, that's all I've been doing for the past few days."

"No, Charles. I mean really pray for him." I agreed, hung up, and walked into the bedroom, asking Mike if I could pray for him. He muttered something unintelligible so I took it as a yes. I grabbed

35

his cold hand, fell to my knees, and prayed with all my might. Tears came from deep within my soul. I then felt a strong and evil presence in the room with us, and it occurred to me that Mike was in a spiritual battle for his life. I remembered reading somewhere that intercessory prayer can be a combination of beseeching the Lord and rebuking the enemy. Those words suddenly took on real meaning for me. I stood to my feet, still holding on to Mike's hand as though for dear life. I felt like if I let go, he'd drift away like an unanchored canoe. I then rebuked the enemy in Jesus's name. The change was dramatic and instant. Color returned to his face.

He opened his eyes, said a soft, "Thank you very much," and dozed off into a peaceful sleep.

Mike awakened a few hours later. He was completely well and back to his old self. He called his wife, then Angel, and then Pete. He told them that he had felt like he was slipping into eternity. Way off in the distance, he heard my prayerful voice asking God for mercy and rebuking the enemy on his behalf. Mike told everyone on the other end of the phone line that he was so glad he brought me with him to New York City. That day the Lord called me into an intercessory prayer ministry!

A few days later, Mike treated me to lunch at a great Puerto Rican restaurant. Once we were stuffed to our gills with chicken, rice, beans, sweet bananas, and flan, he changed gears and got really serious.

"Charles, I've been prayerfully thinking about something for a few days. I know it seems crazy, and it's certainly not what we planned. I'm not going to force you to do anything you don't feel peace about. But it's something we need to consider. You know my father's apartment is where I stay when I come up for my outreaches. The apartment was free for him because it came with his building superintendent's job. Would you be willing to take over his job and live in his apartment, at least for a little while? I'm sure we could get Pete to come up and be your roommate."

"Mike," I tried to interject, but he just kept talking over me.

"We could try it for a little while, and if you want to go back to the farm, maybe we could eventually let Pete take the super job. My uncle works at the superintendents' union office. He says he can work something out for us. The job also comes with a salary. The apartment has that small backyard, and a full basement, and..."

"Mike, Mike, OK! No need to convince me. The Lord spoke to me a few days ago and told me that this is my new home. He's expanded my mission field from Miguel to all the Tonys and Marias in this city. God has called me to be a missionary to New York City!" I shared with him the vision I had of looking down upon New York on the day I die. I told him about the way *West Side Story* tore my heart to pieces, and the nudging I felt every time I saw the ministry's slide presentation of the hurting people here, and what God spoke to me after watching *The Cross and the Switchblade*.

Mike asked, "Are you afraid of living here in the city, Charles?"

"On my own I would be. But for those who are completely surrendered to God, He gives supernatural courage." Mike was pleasantly shocked at such an answer coming from a young, skinny teenager from Tennessee. No need to tell him that my answer actually was a quote from a David Wilkerson sermon. I was experiencing it for myself. Just as true as when it was first preached by David Wilkerson, God was giving *me* supernatural courage.

3

"God is raising up believers to follow in our footsteps."

MIKE SOON LEFT TO GO BACK TO THE MINISTRY HEADQUARTERS IN TEN-nessee, and Pete had to first tie up some loose ends before he could join me. I then decided to read *The Cross and the Switchblade*, the copy Mike had once given to his dad. I opened it up to the title page and read the cursive script: "Papi, The same God who changed me and the people in this book wants to change your life also. Your loving son, Mike." Angel told me months ago that the book was so much better than the movie. I quickly discovered how true that was! I couldn't put it down. I took it with me everywhere I went.

While reading the book on a subway train to Manhattan, the Lord spoke to me in an amazing way. I got on the number 5 train at the 149th Street Station, located at the busy Hub. As the 5 train headed into Manhattan, it shifted directions from going basically east to west in the Bronx to going north to south in Manhattan. While in this transitional tunnel, the long turn is quite noticeable. The noise of the squeaking wheels filled everyone's ears. Those around me seemed oblivious to it, but the piercing noise sounded like those wheels were screaming. I even wondered if those wheels were about to fall off. I opened the paperback book I simply couldn't put down and continued from chapter 14, where I had left off a few hours earlier:

> One morning, just after I had stepped off the ferryboat at the foot of Manhattan, I walked down the stairs to the subway that would take me over to Brooklyn. The subway at this point makes a great loop, and in the turn, its wheels scream piercingly. This place will always have a special meaning for me. Because it was there, among the screams of the subway, that I suddenly saw my old dream take on substance. It sprang full grown to mind. The house I had dreamed of—we might call it Teen Challenge Center—would be located in the heart of the roughest part of the city.[4]

I closed the book and started weeping as the manifest presence of God fell upon me. I read again:

> The subway at this point makes a great loop, and in the turn, its wheels scream piercingly. This place will always have a special meaning for me.[5]

Suddenly, the turn of the 5 train that I was on was completed, and the wheels stopped screaming. "Lord," I prayed. I was about to continue my prayer with, "Lord, whatever could this mean? What are the chances of my reading this for the first time, reading it at the exact moment I experience the same sounds, caused by essentially the same thing?" My prayer didn't even get that far. When I simply whispered, "Lord," with my eyes closed and tears streaming down my cheeks, His presence upon me intensified. The Holy Spirit spoke gently and clearly to my heart, "You are to follow in the footsteps of David Wilkerson."

"Lord, what does that mean?" No explanation; just an awesome feeling that God was divinely ordering my steps. I finished reading the portion of the book where David Wilkerson described the original vision of Teen Challenge:

> The house I had dreamed of, we might call it Teen Challenge Center: an atmosphere of discipline and affection. Christians living together, working together; a family.[6]

The very night Pete arrived in the Bronx, I told him of the subway incident. I asked him what he thought it might mean for me to follow in the footsteps of David Wilkerson. "That's a no-brainer, Charles," Pete remarked in his frank and friendly New York-Rican way. "Let's see, you're both from a small town. You're both called to preach the Gospel. And you're both sent by God on a mission to New York City. Duh!"

"I guess I'm supposed to be preaching, huh?" Pete's grin meant yes. "With Mike having all the connections, and he's back in Tennessee now, where am I supposed to preach?" I asked.

Pete replied, "I know I'm handsome—but do I look like Jesus to you? Get on your knees in prayer, man. Ask Him where He wants you to preach."

For the next few months, I prayed and prayed and prayed. No phone calls. No pastors knocking down my front door. No conference committees trying to get me as their keynote speaker! But as I waited on the Lord, a faint whisper began to rise from deep within, and it grew a little stronger each day. To my question of, "Lord, where do You want me to preach?" I could hear a faint answer: "The 2, the 4, or the 5."

Then one day I realized that the nearby subway stations had three train lines that came together: the 2, the 4, and the 5 trains. It took another few months before I mustered the courage to stand up in a subway train and say with a thick, slow, southern accent, "Hi y'all. My name is Charles, and I'm from Tennessee. Since y'all are trapped in this subway car with me for the next 120 seconds, you are forced to listen to my little sermonette." However, an amazing thing happened. I chose the 5 train because of its inspirational screaming wheels. The third time I nervously stood up to speak, a dear old saint (an elderly, godly-looking African American woman) whom I had never seen before in my life literally ran over to me. She declared, "Young man, I've been preaching the Gospel on this train for decades. I'm gettin' too old to leave my apartment nowadays. I've been prayin', intercedin', and beseechin' the Lord Jesus to raise up someone to take my place. And you're the one. Here, take my mantle, take my anointing, and boldly proclaim the Good News!"

It looked like she threw her shawl over me, but whatever it was, it was invisible! I didn't even believe in that type of Pentecostal weirdness, yet an unmistakable warmth and supernatural energy flowed down onto my shoulders and into my heart. The next time I stood to give a small sermonette, heavenly authority poured from my surprised lips. Everyone on the train turned their bulging eyes and listened attentively and quietly! That subway car came to a stop between stations for a number of minutes due to track signal problems. It was a sure indication to me that God wanted that group to hear a little more than a sermonette, so I gave them a full sermon!

I soon graduated to subway platforms, where my audience could hear a ten- to twenty-minute sermon, depending on how frequently the trains were running. Pete and I went to Central Park in Manhattan, where I discovered if I stood near a certain lake, my voice bounced off the water and up to all the surrounding hills where multitudes of people were picnicking. One man angrily came down and told me that if I didn't stop, he'd throw me into the lake. I felt the thrill of my first bout of real persecution for Christ. It wasn't being thrown to hungry lions, but it was a start! Frequently, old ladies on the subway attacked me with their purses, often screaming something about being Jewish and not wanting to hear my speeches about Jesus. More often, people would come over to me when I finished, grab my arm, and say, "Please, pray for me."

One day, I finished preaching on the 138th Street subway platform. A man who had been listening for a while introduced himself as the youth pastor of a nearby church. I was thrilled when he asked if I could preach to his youth group the following Friday night. When the time came, Pete and I walked over to the Youth Center on Brook Avenue. Pete remarked, "Man, this is a bad neighborhood—as in really bad."

That evening, I preached on the Great White Throne Judgment, remarking that the word *great* is an adjective describing the word *white*, which in the Greek means "bright" or "shining."[7] The greatness of the brightness of His throne will expose and convince everyone of just how deserving we all are of eternal punishment. Oh, that we would allow God to convince us now so we can obtain His mercy and forgiveness instead! All the kids sitting in the rows in front of me seemed to be believers already so I felt like I was "preaching to the choir." Halfway through the service, I noticed that the front entrance was filled with teenagers straining to hear what I was saying—ten, maybe fifteen of them. I knew it was the anointing of the Spirit that was drawing them so I passionately pleaded with them to come in and accept Christ. Some of the kids in the first few rows came to the altar that night (probably for the hundredth time), but none from the curious group from the outside. It was a bittersweet moment for me.

I got together with this same youth pastor a few days later to talk things over. He said, "Hey, you mentioned you're from Cleveland, Tennessee. Did you know that's where the headquarters of our denomination is?"

"No, I didn't know that" (a statement I had used a lot since coming to that strange new world).

"Yeah, Church of God, Iglesia de Dios," he said. "It's taken a long time to get my credentials with them. Are you licensed with the Church of God?"

"No, I'm not licensed with anyone."

"That's too bad," he remarked. "If you had a Church of God license, I could get you all kinds of preaching engagements."

Pete came home from work one day with an exciting announcement. "Guess who's preaching in Manhattan this Sunday? David Wilkerson! He's doing an open-air meeting at Lincoln Center in the morning; then he's preaching at Glad Tidings Tabernacle in the evening."

"Alright!" I replied. "Isn't that the church that took up the offering that enabled Brother Dave to buy the Teen Challenge house in Brooklyn?"

Pete's startled look said, "How do you know that?"

"I read the book a few months ago. Let's see if we can go to both meetings."

Sunday arrived quickly, and the weather was perfect for outdoor preaching. The subway trains were running slow. By the time we arrived at the outdoor amphitheater right next to Lincoln Center, the singing was ending and Brother Dave was being introduced. I was so ready to hear stories about gangs and drug addicts. Instead, this thin, frail-looking man with dorky sunglasses got up and talked as if he was an uncle who lived on the Upper West Side! He spoke about Lincoln Center, Columbia University, the Planetarium, and Central Park (subjects of interest to Manhattanites but very boring to us Bronxites!). Then he spoke about the sins of cheating on your income taxes, stealing towels from fancy hotels, and watching pornography on television late at night when the family has gone to sleep. Pete yawned in deep boredom, but I turned around and looked at the audience. Wow, what a sight! Tons of middle-aged men, obviously under deep conviction, were fidgeting in their seats, not knowing where to hide.

David Wilkerson then said, "You men are so proud and yet so cowardly that if I give an altar call, you'd all be too chicken to come up here. But the Lord still loves you anyway. When you get home, go to your bedroom, shut the door, get on your knees, and repent of your sins. He'll meet you right there and forgive you. Good afternoon." He shut his Bible with a loud thud and walked away!

Not even those who sponsored the event were expecting such a blunt ending. They weren't prepared to come up for a closing song. It took five awkward minutes for them to respond, and yet in those long minutes, conviction rose to such a level that I saw many people's eyes tearing up. Some had their heads bowed, not knowing where to hide.

I turned back around and leaned back into my seat and simply said, "Wow!"

Pete looked at me with anger and replied, "Wow is right! I am so disappointed. David Wilkerson is boring. That was the dumbest message I've ever heard."

"No, Pete, you've got it all wrong. It was actually brilliant. He didn't come here to entertain these people. He came to preach to them what they needed to hear. Look at all the guys walking out of here without talking to anyone. There's such deep conviction in the air. Brother Dave tailored his message to his audience. Can't you see that? These people wouldn't relate to gangs and switchblades."

Pete shrugged his shoulders and said, "I hope he's more anointed tonight."

At Pete's insistence, we spent most of the afternoon standing in front of Glad Tidings in the hopes of meeting Brother Dave face to face. Finally, five minutes before the meeting was to start, Brother Dave and Don Wilkerson came walking up the street. Pete boldly jumped right in front of them and announced, "Brother Dave! My name's Pete, and this is Charles. We're part of an evangelistic ministry, and we're called to minister in the Bronx. Charles is from Tennessee, and I'm from Spanish Harlem. We've been so blessed by your ministry and movie. We've shown it all over the Bronx and all over Tennessee!"

"Nice to meet you guys," Brother Dave said. He politely shook our hands and then walked into the church. Pete kept talking as though he was still standing there. I nudged him with my elbow and said, "Let's go find some seats. The music has started."

The place was crowded, yet the entire front row was empty—a common occurrence when bigwigs speak in churches in case they bring their whole team with them. Pete marched to the front and plopped himself down on the front row as though he was with the speaker. I sat down next to him. Brother Dave's message was fiery, Pentecostal, and great! Nothing mild about the sermon or its delivery!

Pete leaned over and whispered in my ear, "Is this the same guy we saw earlier today?"

"No, it's his twin brother, who even dresses exactly like him."

Brother Dave looked down at us, and I wondered if he was about to rebuke us for talking while he was preaching. Instead, he used us as an illustration to drive home a sermon point. "See these two young men on the front row? That's Pete from Harlem and Charles from Tennessee. They both have been called by God to preach the Gospel in this great city. I'm so glad God is still calling and raising up young believers to carry on His work in this place and to follow in our footsteps."

We could hear many hearty "amens" rising from the lips of those in the audience, many of whom were clearly senior citizens, people who had labored in this city even before Brother Dave was born. All I could think was, "Oh my, there are those words again, 'Walking in the footsteps of David Wilkerson,' and this time, they're coming from the horse's mouth!"

4

"Get things right privately, or God will have to do it publicly."

THE NEED TO GO THROUGH MINISTERIAL LICENSING WITH A DENOMINA-tion soon became even more apparent to me. Reality of Life Ministries crumbled after the leader's marriage tragically disintegrated. Although its members were the vessels the Lord used to save and disciple me, the thought of being a part of a stable denomination became quite appealing. The bitter pain of disappointment from my spiritual leaders was magnified by a long and hard season that I personally went through, which would take another book even to summarize. That's another story for another time. Besides, family members involved still need healing. I know they would prefer me to wait before I share our story. (No man is an island unto himself.)

I spoke with one of the leaders of the Church of God in charge of credentialing in Cleveland, Tennessee, and was quite frank; the good influences of New York City's culture were finally rubbing off on me.

"Pastor, there's one thing in your doctrinal statement that I have problems with." He smiled and slowly nodded his head up and down as if he knew where I was heading. "I've enjoyed the feet washing services in which I've participated, but I don't think it's a church ordinance like water baptism and communion are."

He leaned back in his large leather chair and slowly said, "I know. Actually, there are not that many of us who would disagree with you on this."

"But I have to say on the ordination application that I agree with it?"

"I'm afraid so, young man. Maybe one day our denomination will change that part of its doctrinal statement. Maybe."

Again I was quite frank, responding, "So for me to be ordained with the Church of God, I would have to begin the process by lying? I can't do that." I rose up and walked out of his office, immediately wondering if I had been too blunt. The Assemblies of God's doctrinal statement was very similar to the Church of God's, except they don't teach feet washing as an ordinance. Therefore, I decided to go that route. Their credentialing process required a Bible college degree. I prayerfully decided to move to Baton Rouge, Louisiana, and attend Jimmy Swaggart Bible College, the most on-fire AG school in the nation at the time. Despite problems that would affect the ministry later, in my opinion it was the most amazing place on the planet in 1987. I speak as a student who lived on campus and an employee who worked in the administrative building (as a night custodian). If you thought the telecasts were good, in person the awesome presence of God was overwhelming! And I'll tell you why.

I arrived on a Saturday to begin classes the following week. I was told there would be a prayer meeting in the main sanctuary that evening. Brother Swaggart was having a meeting in one of the largest stadiums in South America the next day. We (students and employees) were encouraged to come and pray for it. I expected forty, fifty people, maybe even a hundred. When I walked through the doors of the large church, my mouth dropped open as I witnessed hundreds of people around the altar. Perhaps over a thousand people were there. Some were in their seats, but everyone was praying as though their own unsaved moms were going to be in that stadium tomorrow. Many of those intercessors were white- and silver-haired senior citizens. I'd never seen anything like it, before or since. Throughout the course of the school year, every time a prayer meeting was called on campus, if you didn't get there early, you couldn't even get in. I don't know how it came about, but by the time I arrived in Baton Rouge, Brother Swaggart had an actual army of intercessors who covered every aspect of his ministry with fervent prayer. Is it any wonder the presence of God was so thick there? It felt like you could slice it.

During one chapel service, a missionary shared about the garbage people in Mexico City. They literally live on top of a garbage dump. For the first time in my life, I heard about people who were even needier than the homeless and destitute who wander the lonely streets of New York City. "Lord, maybe I should go there instead." No. Deep inside, I knew that as soon as I was done with Bible college, I'd be back in New York City.

I went to the singles' meeting one Friday night. During the singing part of the service, I sensed the Lord giving me a prophetic word to share. In the Pentecostal circles in which I was trained, prophecy rises from within the heart of a believer much like lava flows out of an erupting volcano: powerful, spontaneous, and intense! I knew from previous meetings they allowed such things, so at the end of the last song, I stood up and spoke.[8]

The singles' pastor was so excited. In a ninety-second utterance, I touched on every single point of the message he was about to teach. He actually had his outline printed on a transparency, so when he showed it to the group by way of the overhead projector, gasps filled the room and everyone knew God was clearly speaking through both the prophetic word and the sermon. He shook my hand at the end of the meeting and thanked me for my obedience and boldness in bringing forth such a confirming word. The next Sunday, someone brought forth one of those "volcanic" words in the main service.

Over five thousand people were in attendance. However, it was fleshly, man exalting, and clearly not from God. It included words like, "This is the greatest ministry the world has ever known." The Holy Spirit exalts Christ, not men or ministries.

I was so grieved that on my walk across campus afterward, I prayed about it. "Lord, let the gifts of the Holy Spirit come forth in this church with purity and clarity."

He spoke to my heart saying, "Let Me use you."

"No way, Lord. I could never stand in front of thousands of people and bring forth a prophetic word."

"If you're not willing to be part of the solution, then stop praying about it," He said.

A few weeks later, another confusing, crazy, so-called prophetic word was spoken. "OK, Lord. If You want to use me in this area, I'm available."

The following Sunday, Brother Swaggart was away in another Central American city. There was a guest speaker that morning, and the assistant pastor was officiating. The place was packed. Toward the end of what seemed to be the last song, I sensed the rumbling of that volcano in my spirit.

"Charles, stand up at the end of this song and bring forth a word," I heard the Lord say.

"What do I say, Lord?" (Sometimes I get bits and pieces, or the opening statement ahead of time.)

"Stand up now and say, 'Thus says the Lord,' and I'll then give you the rest," He answered.

"Oh, Lord," I sighed as the song ended and nobody moved. Nobody moved for an entire two minutes, an eternity in a church service.

Again I heard, "Stand up now and say, 'Thus says the Lord,' and I'll give you the rest."

"OK." I closed my eyes, stood to my feet, and bellowed out, "Thus says the Lord...because iniquity abounds in this ministry, I am about to remove My anointing. I am the Lord of My Church, and I am the One who walks among the seven golden candlesticks. This has been a candlestick church, but that shall change, for I see everything..."

"EXCUSE ME," the assistant pastor yelled over me from the pulpit microphone. "EXCUSE ME, BROTHER. YOU ARE IN YOUR FLESH. SIT DOWN NOW AND BE QUIET. Let's sing another song."

I opened my eyes. There I was, standing in the midst of thousands of people: co workers, fellow students, teachers, friends, and strangers. The most embarrassing moment of my life. I sank down into my chair and wished I could melt into the floor. I didn't hear any of the announcements or much of the sermon. All I heard were the verses in the Bible that declare, "Woe to those who say, 'Thus says the Lord,' and the Lord has not spoken."[9] I thought about those times in New York and Tennessee when I stood up and gave what I thought was a word from God. Was I off then, too? How could I be so deceived? What about the message to the singles' group outlining the pastor's sermon? How could that be of God and this not be God? Same feelings and same promptings. I was utterly confused. I was the first one to the altar when the preacher gave a call for salvation or for backsliders to repent. "Lord," I cried, "if I'm somehow deeply deceived into bringing forth false words, I am so very, very sorry."

Someone tapped me on my right shoulder, and I was surprised to see white-haired Brother Jones, the head of the Senior Citizen's Intercessory Group. I raised my weeping head up from the altar floor. He bent down and whispered into my ear: "Young man, that was one of the clearest prophetic words I've ever heard, very similar to the word that came forth in our last elders' meeting here in the church. It was from God. You were not in your flesh."

I looked over at the assistant pastor who had rebuked me. Which one of those two leaders was right? "Lord, You say in Your Word that when prophecies come forth, the elders are to judge it.[10] These elders are not in one accord. I'm going to get up now and walk out of here. If it was of God, have another elder stop me and confirm it before I get to the back door. Otherwise, I'm leaving here and never coming back, and I'll never speak prophetically again."

I didn't take two steps before another gray-haired elder stopped me. He also told me that the word was from God, then another, and another. One of the teachers and then a few of the students stopped to encourage me as well. It took me half an hour to get to the back of the church.

The next day I made an appointment with the assistant pastor to discuss the situation. He was extremely kind and treated me with great respect. He remembered who I was so we didn't have to reiterate awkwardly what had happened at Sunday's service.

"Charles, we have a policy here. If we don't know who you are, the first time you bring forth a word, we shut you down. And judging your reaction to that, we then allow or disallow future words."

I was flabbergasted by his explanation and didn't know how to process it. I quickly changed the subject and started talking about New York City, Mike's ministry, and David Wilkerson.

Pastor Rintz got up, leaned on the edge of his desk, and took a good long look at me. He said, "Charles, I like your spirit. You can bring forth any words you'd like to from now on. And if you finish the pastoral program here, this ministry will financially support your work in New York City when you return." I left the ministry office flying high yet bewildered over their shut-the-first-timers-down policy.

The following week, Brother Swaggart's telecast highlighted the awesome ministry of Bill Wilson. His outreach to the kids in Brooklyn was one of the largest Assemblies of God Sunday schools in the nation. As I watched, the burden for New York City broke my heart all over again. I announced to my roommate that I was thinking of leaving for New York sooner than I had planned. The next day, I came back down to reality and realized that in two years I could finish the pastoral degree program and then go back with the blessing and financial backing of Jimmy Swaggart Ministries. Yet, in my prayer closet, tears for lost New Yorkers flowed. I told my roommate I had to go soon. In a few days, I changed my mind again. Exasperated, he finally said to me, "Charles, why don't you fast and pray and really hear from God before you drive us both crazy?"

I went on the longest fast of my life. I still had to work full-time and attend classes so it was quite trying. On the last day of the fast, I realized that God had graciously given me eight solid confirmations. Not only was I to return to New York City, but I also was to quit school at the end of the semester and leave immediately after. As an employee and student, all my spare money was put into a special account. The school would graciously match my funds, enabling me not to have to work full-time throughout my specific program of study. I had to get approval from the dean of students to withdraw money prematurely.

When I spoke with him, he bluntly said, "Some young men get very stirred up about ministry, don't they? If the Lord is telling you to do as you say, He would really confirm it."

"Sir, if you have fifteen minutes, I have quite a few confirmations to share with you." He escorted me to his office, and we chatted for over an hour. I shared with him about how much the telecast about Bill Wilson's ministry touched me. I shared various Scriptures I received in prayer, along with many other confirmations. For instance, on the last day of my fast, a stranger laid his hands on me in the sanctuary while I was praying about the South Bronx, and he told me that six months after arriving there, I would be pastoring a church in the place I was praying about right then. I told the dean that when I first drove into Baton Rouge, I heard this verse on my car radio from a Christian station: *"...stay there until I bring you word..."* (Matt. 2:13). That was the verse spoken at chapel that morning. It was time to return to my land of promise just as Joseph, Mary, and Baby Jesus did.

The dean was very entertained, blessed, and impressed. "Wow," he finally replied. "You told the truth. That's a lot of solid confirmations alright. I'll release your money, and if you're ever led back here, you're always welcome."

We shook hands at the entrance of his office. He added, "Oh, by the way...one thing to keep in mind: God supernaturally confirms things when He knows we'll need those confirmations for the battles ahead. You'll probably need each one of them to endure the opposition you'll face."

I prayed about his sobering comments, and the Lord spoke to me, saying, "When you turn your heart toward ministering in the South Bronx, you will see the face of satan." I didn't know what He meant by that, but I supposed I'd find out soon enough.

Before leaving Bible college, David Wilkerson was invited to come and minister. He spoke a strange message on Samson and Delilah, surely geared toward us students who would be tempted to destroy our calling by sexual sins. Apparently, the message wasn't just for us students. A few weeks later, one of my fellow employees at Jimmy Swaggart Ministries told me that Brother Swaggart received a letter from David Wilkerson.

"Brother Dave gave him a prophetic word: 'Shut the ministry down for a year and get things right between you and the Lord privately, or God will have to do it publicly.'"

"What was his response?" I asked.

"He said, 'I can't do that. This ministry is too valuable to the Kingdom of God for me to do that.' Charles, did you know that a huge chunk of the senior class is leaving at the end of December? They've been here three and a half years and now they all feel called to go back home. They're not going to graduate. What's happening? Something catastrophic is in the air. I know why you're leaving, but why are so many others suddenly going back home or transferring to other colleges?"

"I don't know," I replied. "I do know it's time for me to go."

5

"Do you have a daily prayer life?"

THE WINTER OF 1987 WAS EXTREMELY COLD IN THE NORTHEAST. IN Baton Rouge, it was short-sleeve weather. In the first week of January, I painfully sold or gave away almost all of my cherished Christian books. I sold my dependable Chevy Nova, packed up all I owned into two large suitcases, bought a one-way Greyhound bus ticket to Manhattan, and said goodbye to my college buddies. When I arrived at the Port Authority in Manhattan, I'd been on that bus for over a day and a half. A tall, lanky fellow kindly asked if I would like him to carry one of my suitcases up to street level, and I gladly agreed. Wow, this place was more hospitable than I remembered.

When we reached the top, he demanded, "That'll be twenty bucks!"

"What! You're crazy!" But *I* was crazy to think he was just being polite, so I pulled out a five-dollar bill and reluctantly gave it to him. A friend in the Bronx had said I could stay with him. He forgot to inform me that the boiler recently broke in his building so his basement apartment was nothing more than a large freezer. I was grateful for a place to stay, but I knew it would only be temporary when he said that if I used an electric heater, the Con Edison bill would be more than he could afford.

The next day, I couldn't wait until it was time to attend Times Square Church's warm Tuesday evening service. The church was a few weeks old and had just moved to a semi-permanent place in the Nederlander Theatre. It was on 41st Street, also known as "Crack Alley." Crack addicts gathered there at night to get high, leaving the sidewalk littered with glass pipes and other paraphernalia. I arrived an hour early and had a great time getting to know Wally and Alex, the men in charge of the building. We became instant friends.

Before the service began, Pastor Dave was sitting up on the stage. He came over to the edge to greet the people in the front row. I was a few feet away so I stood up, and he reached out his hand to me. I said, "Pastor Dave, I met you years ago at Lincoln Center and Glad Tidings Church. Remember? I just came here from Jimmy Swaggart Bible College. The Lord brought me back to the city, just like he brought you back!" Right when I began speaking, the loud music started. I didn't know if he heard a word I said. Pastor Dave smiled and made his way back to his seat. Oh well. In spite of that, we had a wonderful communion service.

Afterward, I asked, "Hey Wally, that hallway above the balcony sure would make a good prayer room. You mind if I come by tomorrow and spend some time up there praying?"

"No problem. You can come anytime and stay as long as you want. Maybe I'll join you tomorrow for a little while. Just ask for me when you come, and I'll let you in." I came on Wednesday, Thursday, and Friday! Not only was it a great place to pray, but also it was so nice and toasty. Besides, every time I asked what He wanted me to do, the Lord prompted me to focus in on prayer. So that's what I did. I soon completely ran out of money. One of my new friends, named Bill, could surely sympathize with me. He had been a professional window installer. He fell into a crack addiction that ruined his life and reduced him to being a homeless addict. He found his way somehow to the Bowery Mission, where he was saved and discipled.

He completed their nine-month program and then joined Times Square Church.

"Hey Charles, I'm staying in a place called Baby Step Mission in the Bronx [not the real name]. It's for people coming out of drug programs or prison. You get a free room and meals. I'll ask if you can stay there for a while. They have a one-year limit, but I'm sure things will open up for you. Times Square Church even supports them on a monthly basis because they sometimes take in homeless people who get saved here."

Bill got permission for me to stay there temporarily. However, there were no empty beds so all they could offer me was to sleep on the floor of Bill's tiny room. At least it was warm, and there were meals. Well, kind of. There was a kitchen and we were welcome to cook and eat whatever we could find in the cabinets. All that was left in those cabinets were three items: oatmeal, canned beef stew, and peanut butter. Day after day after day we cooked oatmeal or beef stew. We got creative and had a choice of regular oatmeal or peanut butter-flavored oatmeal. It actually is quite good, and it sticks to your ribs during cold winter days.

After the next service, Pastor Dave shook my hand again and asked me where I was staying. I was a little embarrassed to say, but when he asked you something with those piercing eyes, lying even slightly was out of the question. "I'm staying at Baby Step Mission in the Bronx."

"We support them financially," he commented. "Is everything OK there?"

"Yes, they're kind people and everything's fine."

Not long after that brief conversation, I found out that everything was not fine. The ministry had another building where the director, her unsaved husband, and the women lived. Word got out that the husband was having sex with a number of those women. They were trapped. If they refused, they'd be out on the streets in

59

no time, with no place to go. That nauseated me. Something had to be done. One of the men in my building, in whom a desperate female tenant had confided, wrote a letter to the ministry board addressing this woman's concerns. I asked if I could attend their monthly ministry board meeting. It consisted of the director, her secretary, and a few local pastors. After they skirted the issue for over an hour, I asked to speak. "Look, you have a wonderful ministry here, helping a lot of people in desperate need, including myself, for which I'm truly grateful. However, you have an unsaved husband who can't or won't control himself. Therefore, you should put all the men in your building and move the women over to the other building."

The pastors all nodded their heads in agreement, and one of them said, "I don't know who this guy is, but he speaks as a prophet."

While the board agreed upon and then voted in my suggestions, I heard the Lord say to me, "Within a few weeks, they will decide to change their minds and keep things exactly the way they are. I want you to leave here then."

The next morning I woke up cold and depressed. I was in no mood to eat oatmeal—regular or peanut butter flavored. I laid on the hard floor and vividly recalled all the supernatural confirmations that had been given to me. Had God really called me back to New York City in the middle of such a harsh winter? My mind went back to my warm, soft bed in the college dorm, and I mentally strolled to the sunny college cafeteria. Happy students ate all they wanted from a yummy breakfast smorgasbord. Eggs, biscuits, bacon, sausage, French toast, pancakes, muffins, cantaloupe, honeydew, orange juice, coffee. Boy, if I missed it, I really missed it big. After the next Tuesday night service was over, however, I was very grateful that I was not in Baton Rouge.

Pastor Dave got up and announced, "Folks, we really need to pray tonight. People all over the world are about to be shocked. Tom Brokaw called me from NBC News and confirmed that another television evangelist has fallen into sin: Jimmy Swaggart." At the same time, six people in the congregation let out a loud, "Noooo," in anguish and shock and pain. I was one of them. I had been an employee, a student, and a member of Family Worship Center. Brother Swaggart was our beloved pastor. (I still love him and wish him and his family the best.)

The next few days, I contacted some friends on campus. They all said the same thing. I was so blessed not to be there. There were ten times more reporters on campus than students—reporters from every major media organization from around the globe. Everywhere you went, someone would stick a microphone in your face and ask you a stupid question, hoping to get a silly remark they could use on the air. If you said anything to those reporters, you were immediately kicked out of the college. A couple of friends reminded me of the word I gave in the main sanctuary a few months back. One friend tearfully said to me over the phone, "Thanks, Charles, for bringing forth that word. Strangely, it's been a real comfort to the shattered student body. It has reminded us that Jesus is still the Lord over His Church, and He sees and knows everything."

A few weeks later, I started feeling really weird. "Lord, I haven't eaten any fresh fruit or vegetables in many weeks, only oatmeal, beef stew, and peanut butter. I hope I'm not coming down with scurvy like those guys in the clipper ship days as they journeyed to America without any fresh fruit. Please, Lord, lead me to a good-paying job somewhere, and maybe one with a signing bonus. I need to buy some vitamin C real soon." I pulled out the classifieds from The *New York Times*. Before I could begin my search, I heard the gentle whisper of God.

"Go to Times Square Church today and spend the day with Me in prayer and worship."

"OK, Lord."

Wally was too busy cleaning to pray, which was fine because I was in desperation mode. I felt like I was at the end of my rope and I needed to cry mightily to the Lord. I was soon pacing back and forth in my warm prayer closet hallway, praying in the Spirit at the top of my lungs. I knew that I didn't have to yell to be heard by God, but the Word does say that even Jesus offered up prayers with strong crying and tears.[11] That's what I felt like doing—offering up prayers to God with strong crying and tears. Wally was vacuuming the sanctuary below. No one could hear me up there anyway, except the One to whom I was crying. "Lord, put it in someone's heart in the congregation to ask if I need a job. Let them ask me tonight, Lord, at the Tuesday evening service. I believe You can do this for me, because I'm at the end of my rope. I feel sick and vitamin deprived. Lord, please help me! Please rescue me!"

I didn't know this until a few days later, but at about 11:00 A.M. Pastor Dave came to the sanctuary on his way to the office. He needed to ask Wally something about the church's boiler. When Wally saw him coming down the aisle, he turned off the loud vacuum cleaner. From the top of the balcony, my voice bellowed out, filling the whole sanctuary.

"What in the world is that?" a startled Pastor Dave asked, looking up and around, trying to figure out from where my voice was coming.

"Oh, that's the guy from Tennessee. Charles Simpson. He comes here often and spends the day up there in prayer. He's alright."

"Oh, OK," Pastor Dave said.

———————— ◆ ————————

The next day I woke up to reality. Although I'd been faithful to obey everything I felt the Lord had put on my heart, my wallet was still empty. My body was hurting. My mind was filled with fears that I would die of scurvy. My eight confirmations all seemed like cruel jokes. No one at church offered me a job, although I spent the whole day fasting and praying and believing God for it. Well, thank God Wally slipped subway tokens into my hands every time he saw me. Otherwise, I'd have had no way of getting around. I reluctantly got up and ironed my one suit, put on one of my two ties, and spit-shined my dress shoes. I started mapping out on a spiral notebook the companies I'd worked for in the past, knowing I'd have a better chance of landing a much-needed job with one of them. Let's see: General Nutrition Center, Nature Food Center, and IHOP. I'd try those places first. I forced myself to eat some beef stew, knowing I might not be home until late. I cleaned my dishes and headed toward the front door. I had to walk past the first floor chapel entrance. When I did, I realized that I actually didn't have a burning desire to spend time with God that morning. Was I upset with Him? Unlike New Yorkers, we southerners sometimes have a hard time getting in touch with our actual feelings, especially if they're feelings we're not supposed to have. I felt the Lord nudging me to put down my notebook and take my coat off and spend time with Him.

As I began to pray, I told Him what was on my heart. "Lord, I'm at the end of my rope. I'm tired and discouraged. I feel like giving up and going home. But Baton Rouge is not my home, and Cleveland, Tennessee, is no longer my home." I began to cry—a little bit at first, but then deep, heavy sobs came gushing out of my utterly downcast soul.

God promises comfort to those who mourn, and I soon felt the manifest presence of the Lord. I heard Him saying to my heart: "Charles, I am your home. Come running to Me." I fell to my knees, and then I got on my face and wept even deeper into the chapel's red carpet on which I was lying. I remembered Jesus's agony in the garden and His prayers to the Father. From the depths of my soul, I cried out, "Abba Father, please help me! Abba Father, please, please help me!"[12]

Suddenly, the carpet on which I was lying on became the bosom of our Heavenly Father. I felt His arms around me and His warm bosom underneath me. He simply held me in His arms as I cried out all my pain.

"I'm your home, My precious son. I'm your home," He whispered over and over to my heart.

I felt like I had a Jabbok experience, similar to when Jacob desperately wrestled with the angel all night. He would not let the angel go until he blessed him.[13] Jacob came out of that encounter with God changed forever. God even changed his name to Israel, for as a prince he struggled in prayer and prevailed. I was ready to go job hunting. I somehow knew God would lead and bless me.

I got off the floor and found my notebook, opening the page I had written on earlier. "Father God," I said out loud, "which one should I try first?"

"Go speak with David Wilkerson today," I clearly heard the Lord say to my heart as if it were my roommate Bill talking to me. I realized that Pastor Dave had asked me about the spiritual condition of Baby Step Mission weeks earlier because he supported it financially and wanted my honest opinion. Since then, I had found out how messed up things really were. "OK, Lord. I guess I do have a responsibility to inform him. I'll do that first." I went out to a phone booth on a cold windy street corner and called Times Square Church's office.

A sweet lady with a very kind voice answered: "Times Square Church! How can I help you?"

"Well, I need to speak with Pastor Dave today about a sensitive issue. I attend the church, and he asked me about a particular ministry that he supports. I originally told him everything's fine here, but it isn't. I need to tell him about it."

"Here's what you do," she replied. "After any of our services—Tuesday evening, Friday evening, Sunday morning or evening—come behind the stage, and Pastor Dave will be glad to speak with you then."

"OK. Thank you." When I hung up, I felt like I wasn't supposed to call. I was supposed to go and speak with David Wilkerson that day. I couldn't shake off the feeling that I needed to speak with him immediately—not Friday, not next Sunday. Well, I had my suit on, and I was ready to head out. I would just stop by the office first and try to speak with him.

That very morning, Pastor Dave went to the church before going to his office to deal with a sticky situation. He and Wally talked things over and realized they needed to hire another person to assist Wally in caring for the facilities.

"Wally, do you have any suggestions as to whom I should hire?"

"Only one, Pastor Dave. That guy from Tennessee. Charles Simpson."

About half an hour later, I walked into a very busy office on the second floor of a building on Broadway and 68th Street. After waiting on line, it was my turn to address the receptionist. I hoped she wasn't the one I had spoken with earlier!

"Hi, can I please speak with Pastor Dave? It will only take about five minutes."

"What's it regarding?"

"A sensitive issue regarding a ministry that Times Square Church supports."

"Young man, aren't you the one I spoke with on the phone this morning?"

"Yes, ma'am."

"What are you doing here? I told you Pastor Dave will speak with you after any one of our services!"

"I know, and I'm sorry if I seem to be rude and non-compliant. I just feel so strongly that I'm supposed to speak with him today about this."

She sighed very deeply, looked down at a calendar in front of her, and said, "He's completely booked until 4:45 this afternoon."

Thinking that would sufficiently deter me, she was shocked when I responded, "That's fine. I'll wait." I sat down on a nearby chair, willing to wait there all day if need be.

Suddenly, the telephone stopped ringing, and the front doorbell stopped buzzing, and all was quiet. The only ones around were the kind receptionist and me. After doodling on her calendar for a while, she looked up and said, "Where are you from?"

I told her that I was from Tennessee and had moved to New York City as a teenager to be a missionary. I told her about hearing Pastor Dave a few years ago at Lincoln Center and meeting him that same day at Glad Tidings. She was noticeably touched when I told her that from that day on, Pastor Dave had been on my daily prayer list, right under the names of my family members. I told her about my time in Bible college and the various confirmations the Lord had given me that I was to come back to the city.

David Wilkerson's office door opened, and he walked out, heading toward the receptionist. She swung around in her swivel chair and enthusiastically said to him, "Honey, you've got to speak with this young man. He's a missionary to New York City from Tennessee. He's been praying for you every day for years!" This lady was Gwen Wilkerson, Pastor Dave's sweet wife.

He shook my hand as though it was the first time and said, "I've got a few minutes before my next appointment. Step into my office."

I walked into a beautiful corner office with glass walls overlooking Broadway. "Have a seat," he said, pointing to a comfortable chair in front of a large mahogany desk. Even before I was seated, he asked, "So what can I do for you?"

"Well, Pastor Dave, it's a sensitive issue."

"I can handle sensitive issues. Get to the point."

"Well, I attend Times Square Church. You asked me a few weeks ago how things are at Baby Step Mission, and I said everything was fine. I now know everything's not fine. I felt I had an obligation to come and tell you."

Pastor Dave leaned forward, looked right into my eyes (and right through my soul), and said, "The director's husband is fornicating with the women in the program, isn't he?"

"Uh, yes. That's what...how do you know this?" He leaned back into his chair and said, "The Holy Spirit just now told me. I'm right, aren't I?"

I nodded my head slowly, realizing I was in the presence of a real, live, honest-to-goodness prophet. I was temporarily frozen with fear and admiration. He jumped to his feet and began to escort me toward the door. I guess prophets don't bother with small talk.

"What's your name again?" he asked.

"Charles Simpson."

"Charles Simpson from Tennessee?"

"Yes, sir."

"Charles, I have a job for you if you're interested. We need another man to assist Wally in caring for the building. It's room and board. Well, it does include a small salary and some benefits. Are you interested?"

"Very interested, sir."

"Good. I'll tell my son Greg to go over the details with you this afternoon. He'll be at the church from four to eight o'clock today. Speak with him about the room backstage you can move into. He can show you where to cook your food and things like that. Oh, before we make this final, I require one thing of every employee of mine. I need to ask you one question. Tell me the truth."

I nodded my head and felt like if I lied, I'd probably drop dead right there. I said to myself, "No matter how much I want this job, I must not lie. I must not lie. I hope it's an easy question. Lord, let it be an easy question."

Pastor Dave once again zeroed in on the back walls of my eyes and asked me, "Do you have a daily prayer life?"

I looked deep into his eyes with confidence and a smile and said, "Yes, sir, I do," like a happy, newly enlisted Marine!

"Good. Welcome aboard!" He finally cracked a smile and shook my hand to seal the deal. "You were at Jimmy Swaggart Bible College last year, weren't you?" he asked.

"Yes, Pastor Dave. I left in January along with much of the senior class. We knew something was wrong. We were told that you warned him to shut things down and get things right between him and the Lord."

"Yes, I spoke briefly with him while I was there. A week or so later I wrote him a three-page warning. I said if he didn't shut things down for a season, then God would have to shut him down completely. He told me he couldn't do that. What a shame," he concluded as he opened his office door to escort me out. I walked into the reception area and shook Gwen's hand. I thanked her exuberantly as tears welled up in my grateful eyes.

Pastor Dave hired me right after I experienced one of the most amazing prayer times of my life. Just as when Jacob, way back in the Book of Genesis, first won the victory in prayer, the outward sign was subsequent favor with man. Jacob soon exclaimed to a smiling Esau, *"I have seen your face as though I had seen the face of God, and you were pleased with me"* (Gen. 33:10). Wow! I was hired to work on staff and to live in Times Square Church!

On the subway ride to the Bronx to get my few belongings, I felt like the Lord was telling me something profound. Because I had looked to my Heavenly Father in a time of total desperation, He was going to bless me with a true spiritual father—one whom I was never to worship, and never dishonor.

6

"When you have authority, you don't have to yell."

LIVING IN TIMES SQUARE CHURCH WAS SUCH A DREAM JOB. I HAD MY own room, plenty of heat, and access to a kitchen stocked with all kinds of food and vitamins! With my small salary, I could even go to the local Christian bookstore and buy one book a week. Yippee! I was soon promoted to an usher, a security guard, and a counselor to assist the busy altar ministry. A few weeks into the job, Greg Wilkerson came down to the church one morning. He found me vacuuming the sanctuary and Wally cleaning the large nursery. Alex had left, and Mark had joined our little crew. Greg gathered us together and asked some specific questions about our various tasks.

He computed hours in his head and said, "This is what my dad would like for you guys to do: get up at the same time, but spend the entire morning in prayer for the various needs of the church. Then you can clean in the afternoons. OK?"

"Sure," Wally replied as the spokesman with the most seniority. "That sounds great! That's the one thing we've been struggling to find time to do lately."

Greg said, "Let's have a word of prayer together." He bowed his head and prayed, "Lord, we thank You for how much You've blessed this church so far, and for bringing faithful workers to help us, and... and..." He stopped and pulled out a handkerchief to wipe away the flowing tears. Such a tender heart Greg has toward the Lord. "Wally," he whispered, "go ahead and close in prayer," as tears kept streaming down his face.

After Greg left, I said to Wally and Mark, "I can't believe this! We're being paid to pray! I've never heard of anything like this in my whole life!"

During one Sunday morning service, I felt a dormant volcano rumbling deep within my spirit. "Oh Lord," I protested, "I don't think I could ever again bring forth a prophetic word in a church service. Not after what happened in Baton Rouge." I made friends with and confided in Pastor Dave's oldest son, Gary, about the gift of prophecy in which I had once operated and how I was terrified of being openly rebuked again.

Gary heard me out fully and said, "Charles, I really feel that the Lord has given you this gift. Let's pray that the Lord heals the hurts and hindrances. If you ever have a word while I'm leading the service, you can bring it forth anytime. And if I feel that it's off, even way off, I'll wait until after the service to discuss it with you privately."

That really freed me up, and the very next Sunday morning I felt the rumblings of this gift within my spirit. I clearly heard the Lord say, "Get up and exhort the church to fast and pray for their loved ones."

"But Lord," I objected as the music died down, "if I stand up and say, 'Thus says the Lord,' Pastor Dave might get up and rebuke me."

The Lord said to me, "If you don't obey Me, I will rebuke you."

When I stood and said, "Thus says the Lord," I sensed the fear of man rolling off me, never to be taken back into my heart again.[14]

The word was, "I am calling this church to fast, a time of fasting and prayer for your loved ones and for this city."

Before I even sat down, Pastor Dave headed to the microphone and said he was planning on exhorting the congregation to fast and pray for our families. He immediately announced a corporate fast for the following Sunday.

On Tuesday evenings, I ushered in the aisle next to the book and cassette tape table. We sold hundreds of recordings of the rich sermons from the three main pastors: Dave; his brother, Don; and Bob Phillips. Word was getting out all over the Tri-State region that there was some great spiritual food there, and not just from Pastor Dave. Pastor Bob was the best Bible teacher I'd ever heard. His knowledge of the Old Testament and how it applies to the New was amazing. Pastor Don's messages were always encouraging and often funny. It's not like he was trying to be a Christian comedian. It happened naturally, spontaneously, and often. Pastor Dave's sermons were like scalpels that cut us open to the core. Pastor Bob then came along and inspected and cleaned out the wound, and then Pastor Don stitched us up and left us in stitches, literally, with his humor and encouragement!

We were getting our share of crazy people, too. One Tuesday evening before the service was about to begin, a small lady walked up to me and began to share her story. "Mister, I need help," she announced as she clung to me. "I have a demon inside of me," she said, the volume of her voice intensifying with every word. "And when I tell people about him, he gets mad and BEGINS TO SCREAM THROUGH ME," she yelled at the top of her lungs.

I pulled her over to a corner, laid hands on her, and began to rebuke the enemy and command him to "GO!" She got even louder so I started praying louder and faster. We were creating a noisy scene! Out of the corner of my eye, I saw Pastor Dave walking through the front door and heading our way, thank God! I stopped and stepped back a bit as the lady just continued screaming.

Pastor Dave walked up to her and said, "Be quiet."

She stopped and looked around at who else was talking to her. She began her speech again, saying, "I have this evil thing in me, and when..."

"Lady," Pastor Dave interrupted, "I said, be quiet. Do you want to be set free?" She nodded her head yes. "Then go sit down right over there on the front row, and don't say a word for the entire service. When the meeting is over, come to the front. We'll pray for you, and Jesus will set you free. OK?"

She nodded her head again and went to her assigned seat like an obedient child.

Pastor Dave turned to me and said with a faint smile, "Charles, when you have authority, you don't have to yell." I nodded my head like another obedient child and went to my assigned usher's seat. After the service, the lady received prayer and was instantly delivered.

It was around this time that the incident with the purse thief and his razor-sharp screwdriver happened. That episode brought to the forefront a deep-seated fear in my heart, a dread of being stabbed and bleeding to death on the streets of New York City. Perhaps I shouldn't have seen *West Side Story* after all!

As Wally, Mark, and I spent more and more time in prayer, the burden for Miguel's neighborhood in the South Bronx grew in my heart. I decided to start prayer walking the South Bronx on my days off. In my heart, I set my face toward the Bronx. I was standing in front of the Nederlander Theatre one afternoon, talking to a sweet lady named Dolores, one of the elderly sisters who faithfully attended the church.

A tourist with a camera and theater brochures in hand walked up and asked me what kind of play this was: "Times Square Church? What's this play about?"

"It's all about Jesus!" I remarked joyfully. "Actually, it's not a play. This is a church that meets in a theater. We have a service tonight at 7:00 P.M. Why don't you join us?"

From the corner of my eye, I saw a man about five feet six inches tall staring at me with pure demonic hatred in his eyes. I glanced at him, looked away, and then glanced back again, and POW! He smacked me in my face as hard as he could. He then ran down Crack Alley, heading toward the Port Authority Bus Station.

My glasses shattered and went flying. A broken piece cut my face an inch under my left eye. Within seconds, my face was covered with blood. "Why did you do that?" I asked as I turned in the blurry direction that my assailant had gone. Standing there bleeding profusely on the streets of New York City, I realized a number of things. I had set my face toward ministry in the Bronx. I had seen pure evil in that poor man's face, like I was looking into the very face of satan himself. Yet the peace of God was pouring down upon me faster than the blood was pouring out. The Lord is peace, and the Lord was with me no matter where I went and no matter what happened to me.[15] Dolores had some nurse's training and kicked into gear. She pulled out a wad of tissues from her purse, applied it to my cut, grabbed my arm, and escorted me into the church. Blood was dripping everywhere. The front of my shirt was soaked.

"Let's wash this off and see how deep that cut is," Dolores said. "If it hit an artery, we need to call an ambulance right away. If it's somewhat deep, we need to take you in a taxi to get stitches. If it's a minor cut, you'll just need a Band-Aid. How are you holding up?"

"Bleeding on the streets of New York City isn't half as bad as I thought it would be. I'm ready to go to the Bronx," I replied.

"What?" Dolores asked with deep concern. "Are you delirious?"

"I'll explain later," I said.

Thank God, I just needed a Band-Aid, although it would leave a permanent scar.

Mark or Wally would accompany me as I walked and prayed throughout the Mott Haven section of the South Bronx. One Saturday afternoon, we took cartoon-filled Chick tracts with us and handed them out. A young Puerto Rican girl, probably a thirteen-year-old acting like she was eighteen, walked past us all dressed up. Her face was caked with tons of makeup. It looked like she was heading to a nightclub. I tried to hand her a tract.

"No thank you," she said, and kept walking.

I responded by saying, "You need Jesus!"

She stopped, spun around, and walked back toward me, looking right into my eyes. She emphatically declared, "Mister, I love Jesus with all my heart. I just can't stand my grandmother's church."

I knew exactly where she was coming from. She was probably saved in her grandmother's church a while back, but the legalism that marked many Spanish Pentecostal churches could be unbearable. She needed a healthy, English-speaking church in her neighborhood, like Times Square Church.

A friend from church named Tommy invited me to do street preaching with him. He would go out to 42nd Street in Times Square on Saturday afternoons. He'd buy a sound permit from the local police precinct so he could use a small amplifier. One week, Tommy announced that he had to be out of town the following Saturday. He already had the sound permit so I told him I'd be glad to fill in for him. I would read aloud a number of verses from the Bible on God's love and mercy and simply explain them to the throngs of people passing by. As I was quoting from John 3:16—*"God so loved the world"*—I sensed a heavy anointing upon me. One thing about anointing—it tends to stir up a hornet's nest. Two things happened at once. A man from a hate-filled cult across the street called the Black Israelites came over with scissors hidden in his pocket. He cut my microphone cord! At exactly the same time, Pastor Dave's secretary, Barbara, was walking by, and she stopped to encourage me.

"You're doing a great job," she said. "Reminds me of another skinny preacher I know from the country," and she winked at me as the walk sign flashed and she proceeded across the busy street.

Wow, to be compared to David Wilkerson...and by his secretary! I was so encouraged that I kept right on preaching for a while, even without a microphone.

I soon asked Tommy if he could help me get my own amplification system so I could preach in the South Bronx. He bought me an entire system, complete with a microphone and carrying case! I started preaching on a weekly basis at the Hub. There were always huge lines of people waiting for twenty minutes or more for various buses. It was a great place for street preaching, especially since half the people in that neighborhood had been to their mother's or grandmother's or aunt's church at some point in their childhood.

One day, a very elderly man slowly, painfully made his way over to me. "Young man," he began, leaning on a wobbly cane, "when I was young, I used to preach at this very spot. Now I'm too old, but I'm glad God raised up someone to take my place. Be encouraged and keep up the good work!"

I was *not* encouraged by his words. They actually discouraged me tremendously. After he left, I stared into space like a baseball pitcher when the umpire calls a ball and everyone knows that it was clearly a strike.

"Oh, great," I finally complained out loud to the Lord. "One day I'll be too old to come out here and minister God's Word."

I heard the Lord speak these thoughts to me: "If you raise up a church in this neighborhood, it could be a witness for Me until I return."

What a concept! But it was more than a concept. It was a calling, an assignment that I knew was from the Lord. As we were cleaning

Times Square Church the next day, I shared my heart with Wally. "I love my job here, Wally, but I feel the Lord is calling me to the South Bronx to pioneer a new church."

"You need to tell the leadership here about this, Charles."

The following Tuesday evening before the service, I walked up to Pastor Don and told him I'd like a word with him.

"Sure, Charles," he said in his cheerful manner. "What is it?"

"Well, I've been praying over the South Bronx for a number of months. I've been doing street preaching there and...I feel the Lord is calling me to start a church there."

He just stared at me, speechless, for at least sixty long seconds. Was he holding back a hearty round of laughter? Did he think I was joking? Was he thinking, "You? Plant a church in the South Bronx? A young, white guy going to one of the most dangerous parts of this entire region? Are you crazy?"

Instead, he finally, carefully responded, "This is interesting."

"What is?" I asked.

"Just today we pastors had a meeting about what evangelistic outreaches we should have this summer. We're a fairly new church, and we need to have something, but we're not ready to do a lot. After praying together about it, we unanimously decided to have one major outreach this summer...in the Bronx. Since you've been praying for the Bronx, why don't you pick the neighborhood?"

I was so pleasantly stunned that I couldn't even talk. I nodded my head and went to my usher's post as the service began. Pastor Jimmy Lilley, the outreach pastor, picked the date for the Bronx meeting. It wasn't until he told me that I realized it was six months *to the day* from when I arrived back in the city.

A couple days later, Pastor Dave approached me and said, "Charles, since you're called to start a church in the Bronx and we feel led to have an outreach there this summer, let's make it the kick-off for your church. My son Gary will be happy to help you."

Pastor Gary was very excited and offered to help me find a store-front where we could begin our new church. He loves grassroots stuff, and he also has a way of believing in those who don't usually get nominated "Most Likely to Succeed," like skinny white guys from Tennessee. Gary believed in me—really believed in me—and that meant the world to me. Gary said the budget would be one thousand dollars per month for church rent. Times Square Church would generously pay for an apartment for Mark and me in the Bronx. (I needed someone with me who could swat down screwdrivers and switchblades.) They would also give me enough of a salary to live on so I could focus on the new church. What a way to plant a church—a strong mother church fully supporting a daughter church in the same region!

Pastor Gary and I found a small storefront a block from the Hub, right next to a large empty department store. The storefront was going for a thousand a month, but Gary was immediately interested in the much bigger place next door. The real estate broker said the department store was vacant and would remain that way for the next year because Con Edison was eventually buying the entire building. Nobody was going to fix up a department store just for a one-year lease. Pastor Gary asked, "And what's the market price for this department store if it came with a ten- or twenty-year lease?"

The broker said, "Well, it's got two bathrooms, a large front room, three small rooms in the back, and it has its own heating and A/C units. I'd say about ten thousand a month."

Gary responded, "And it's just going to sit here empty for a year?"

"Yep. We're going to have to board it up so no one breaks these large department store windows."

"Tell the landlord we'll take it for a thousand a month. He won't have to board it up, and in a year, he'll have a nice newly-painted space to give to Con Ed," Gary offered.

"The landlord isn't interested in such small change," the broker insisted, "and he doesn't care about fixing things up either. Con Ed has already agreed to buy it as is. OK, I'll ask him anyway. Won't hurt."

A few days later, we had a one-year lease for the large space and we were cleaning and painting it, getting it ready for our opening service in a few weeks.

Two weeks before our street rally, we had an unusually powerful Friday night service at Times Square Church. When Wally, Mark, and I finished doing a security check of the building, we met back at the altar. We all clearly sensed the lingering presence of God. "Let's pray for a while," Wally remarked, and soon we were soaring in prayer together. Before we knew it, it was 3:00 A.M. When I told Wally how late it was, he replied, "I'm not even tired. Let's turn off all the sanctuary lights and keep praying up in your room, Charles." All three of us were praying in the Spirit, and we alternated between praying whatever was on our hearts and singing some of the songs from our services.

I kept getting a picture of a huge Apollo spacecraft mounted on a launching pad, steam billowing out of its sides, ready to shoot up into the heavens. Our prayers soon were 100 percent focused on the Bronx. We interceded about all aspects of the coming street rally and the new church plant. Time flew by, and it was a good thing that nothing was on the calendar for that Saturday. We never did open the church doors. We knew the sun had come up, but still I was surprised when I looked at my watch and saw that it was already noontime! We kept praying and singing and waiting on God, sensing that He was doing something powerful through our intercession.

That evening, all three of us finally stopped praying at exactly the same time. We sat quietly for a few minutes, waiting to see if the Lord was definitely finished. Finally, Wally said, "Man am I hungry!" We all looked at our wristwatches and were amazed to realize it was past 9:00 P.M.! We had prayed for almost twenty-four hours, but it seemed like just a few hours.

Again, Wally spoke up. "Charles, let's go to the deli around the corner on Seventh Avenue and get some sandwiches. Mark, you want anything?"

"No thanks. I have leftovers down in the kitchen."

We got our sandwiches and exited the deli. I said to Wally, "Hey, let's go over to the corner of 42nd Street for a minute." Wally didn't even bother to ask why. He had been with me when I suddenly began preaching or singing or talking boldly about the Lord in public places.

Before we had even arrived at the corner of Seventh Avenue and 42nd Street, I saw a short Hispanic-looking man handing out tracts to whomever wanted to grab one as they briskly walked past him. He turned around and faced me as though he'd been waiting there for me and then said in perfect English, "Thus says the Lord, I have called you and anointed you and appointed you for the work ahead. Do not be afraid as you walk through this new and open door of ministry that I, your Lord, have opened for you. Be bold and courageous, for I am surely with you wherever you go."[16]

My mouth hung open, and I turned to Wally and exclaimed, "Wally, did you hear that? This man doesn't know me from Adam, and..." I turned back toward the street preacher, and he was gone! Could he have jumped into a taxi? Did he run away? Was he a missionary in Mexico who was transported there and back, like Philip, just to give that message to me?[17] Was he an angel? I think so, but I don't know for sure. I knew that the prophetic word was from God. I would go forth to the South Bronx, one of the most dangerous neighborhoods in the world, and I would not be afraid, for God was surely with me!

The street meeting was awesome. We got permission from the mayor's office and the police department to close off an entire city block on 143rd Street, between Third Avenue and Morris. We brought out a stage, a church organ, and the entire Times Square Church worship team. When we put out a hundred folding chairs, the kids in the neighborhood immediately filled them. I saw people coming to their windows from all the housing projects on that block. The worship team sang their hearts out, and Pastor Jimmy preached a very strong evangelistic message. He had a specific altar call for anyone who would like to accept the Lord as their Savior. "Don't come if you don't mean business. Don't come if you've been saved before. This is only for first-timers."

I was thinking, "Jimmy, if you keep narrowing it down, no one will come." But he knew what he was doing, and seventeen people responded. All of them were clearly ready to accept the Lord as their Savior.

At the end of the meeting, Jimmy announced that in two days, where the old Lynn's Department Store used to be, a new church would begin. It would be called the South Bronx Church and I would be the pastor. I began to make my way up to the stage to give my greetings and close in prayer. Someone in the vast crowd yelled out, "You mean that vacant store right beneath the Social Security office around the corner from the Hub?" Jimmy quickly looked over at my nodding head and said into the mic, "Yes, the new church is located near the Hub, underneath the Social Security office." Everyone there knew exactly where to go on Sunday. Jimmy announced, "Pastor Charles, come and greet your new congregation."

I looked down at the seventeen people who got saved. I saw hundreds of men, women, boys, and girls behind them and simply said, "Let's pray." I prayed with all my heart for the families and the homes and the people of the South Bronx and asked for God's richest blessing upon each one. Hearty "amens" filled the air as the meeting came to a wonderful conclusion.

7

"That's exactly what I would have done!"

AFTER PRAYERFUL CONSIDERATION, WE DECIDED TO START OUR SUNDAY services at three o'clock in the afternoon. Was I surprised when fifteen of those first-timers at the street rally showed up, along with sixty people from Times Square Church! It turned out that most of those sixty people came from far away, attended the mother church in the morning, and would usually hang out in restaurants until the 6:00 P.M. service. Back then, they had not yet started their 3:00 P.M. service. It worked out well for everyone.

A year later, our attendance was still about seventy-five people, but by then about sixty were from the neighborhood and only fifteen from Times Square Church. Once we took off, every few weeks or so a Times Square Church member would leave, telling me they had been there just to help us launch—but not without a hug and a big thank you from me. I'm convinced that a mother church birthing a daughter church in a different part of the region is the ideal way to plant a church. As I looked back, I saw so many situations where we really did not know what we were doing. But as Pastor Don said in one of his classic sermons, "It's easier to steer a moving car than a stationary one!"

Our second Sunday was a hot, humid June day, and the Lord put on my heart to preach a sermon about the fires of eternal hell. As we opened the building and turned on the air conditioning units, they made a loud noise and died on us. No air conditioning! Not only did it feel like hell when it was time to preach, but I preached too long. A few times in the middle of that sermon, I commented on how the Lord was allowing us to feel what I was preaching about! But preaching over an hour and a half? It was miraculous that anyone came back the following Sunday! Dolores discreetly walked up to me in the beginning of that next service and asked me how many sermons I was going to preach—two or three? I got the message and tried my hardest to limit it to just one.

Gary insisted I join the weekly pastoral staff prayer meetings, so when I walked into the 68th Street office, Pastor Dave greeted me with a firm handshake. He said, "A friend gave me a cassette copy of your message on hell. A very good sermon. Also, Charles, I know my limitations, and I need to stay focused on what's going on here in Manhattan. My son Gary says he'd love to preach for you on Wednesday evenings, but don't expect me to help you in the Bronx."

"I totally understand, Pastor Dave. And that would be awesome to have Pastor Gary help me." So, for many Wednesday evenings, Pastor Gary preached for me and then sometimes treated me to dessert at a nearby diner. How wonderful it was to spend quality time with him. I could openly discuss the many challenges I was facing there in the Bronx. When he later moved to England, local pastors Mark Gregori and Ben Torres often gave me valuable advice. But neither one was able to be hands-on like Gary was, so when I subconsciously tried to copy the mother church in everything, it only led to frustration and exhaustion. I was trying too hard to follow Pastor Dave and Times Square Church's example. I was trying to follow in Abraham's footsteps by unnecessarily becoming a desert-dweller just like him!

But, thank God, I had such a great assistant in Mark. When he got married to a sister from Times Square Church and moved on, immediately the Lord brought Samuel Henry along. Samuel was an anointed keyboardist from England. His family was originally from the Caribbean, and his father pastored a church in Hempstead, Long Island. Since Samuel was just out of high school and spent so much time traveling back and forth, I invited him to move in with me and told him that he could have Mark's old room. After praying a lot about it and discussing it with his family, he agreed.

Soon after he moved in, suddenly all the people who sat out on the stoops of their buildings in my neighborhood were unusually friendly with me as I walked by. I had to find out why.

"Yo, what's up?" I said to some of the guys on my block, trying to sound urban—except my southern accent was still coming through, kind of messing it all up. "I've been living here for months, and you guys hardly give me the time of day. As soon as Samuel moves in with me, I'm suddenly everyone's friend. What's up with that?"

"Well, it's like this, white boy. Now we know you aren't prejudiced."

"And how do you know that?" I asked.

"You got a black man living with you!"

"I do? Oh yeah, I guess I do! I never thought about it. He's my brother in Christ, and he's on staff at my church, so naturally I offered for him to live with me."

"Pretty cool, white boy. Pretty cool."

Actually, one of the coolest things about having Samuel around was the fact that often at the end of my sermons, God would give me spontaneous songs. Samuel could immediately join in and play along on the keyboard. We flowed together in the heights of Zion and tasted realms of glory that are indescribable.[18] But afterward, we would walk out of glorious meetings, right into the hard, gritty, dangerous streets of the South Bronx. But I was glad I was there, and I knew I was both sent by God and protected by God.

One evening, while eating dinner with a family from my church who lived in the Patterson Housing Projects, gunshots erupted right outside the window. Although we were on the ninth floor, the loud popping sounds were deafening. After a few silent minutes passed, we all ran to the windows and saw a young man lying in a big pool of his own blood. The police sirens began to wail, and because the 40th Precinct was only blocks away, by the time I ran down the steps, the police had already taped off the crime scene.

When I ducked under the yellow tape and approached the body, one officer yelled, "Hey, get away from there!"

Another officer who knew me said, "No, it's OK. Let Father Simpson give him his last rites." It wasn't time to explain that I was a pastor and not a priest so I nodded my head in agreement and got on my hands and knees next to the young man. He had been shot in the back of his head at point-blank range, and his brain was oozing out into the huge pool of blood in which he was lying. It smelled like rotten eggs—the most horrible sight and smell I've ever experienced. To this day, I don't know if the rotten smell was his brain or the sulfur from the gunshot. The young man was barely breathing. I knew he was quickly dying. I knelt down even closer and spoke right into his ear. "Brother, my name is Pastor Charles, and you're about to die. A thief on a cross next to Jesus prayed while he was dying, and he made it into Heaven. That same Jesus brought me here now to lead you in prayer to accept Him as your own personal Savior. Please repeat after me, 'Dear God in Heaven...'"

The young man moved his lips and began to say the word "Dear," but he only got the "D" sound out, "Dah," and his head moved slightly as he breathed his last breath and died.

I stood up and noticed my feet and hands were covered in his blood. I shouldn't have, but in shock, I stared down at him as the rest of his brain oozed out of that huge wound to the back of his skull. A few long moments later, a veteran cop, who probably knew I was in deep shock, grabbed me by the shoulders and escorted me away from the horrible scene.

I couldn't sleep for days. Whenever I would close my eyes, I would see that poor boy's brain coming out of his head. I found out through the grapevine that he was only eighteen. He was dealing drugs and was too slow at paying his suppliers so they made an example out of him. Finally, while deep in prayer one night, I pictured that same young man in Heaven, tapping me on my shoulder and saying to me, "Thank you so much for coming to my neighborhood. Thanks for leading me in the sinner's prayer that night." Is the "D" of "Dear Lord, forgive me of my sins and be my Savior" enough? I believe so. I hope so.

I experienced just as many blessings as tragedies in my first pastorate in the South Bronx. For instance, the highlight of my week wasn't when I stood in the pulpit and preached God's Word to all the hearty "amens" of my vibrant congregation. It happened about five minutes after the service was completely over, just enough time for an usher to tell the Sunday school teacher that the adult service was finished and the kids could come back into the main sanctuary. When that door opened, out came approximately thirty precious children. And of those thirty, only one had a father at home. The other dads were either in jail, dead, or only God knows where. I was a substitute father to those kids, and we greeted each other with hugs and high fives and with them showing me all the crafts they had made in class.

Another highlight was our Halloween service, which we named "Free Movie Night." We decided to offer free candy, popcorn, and soda to the kids in the neighborhood at the conclusion of showing the film *The Cross and the Switchblade*. Although we handed out thousands of fliers the weeks before, when it was time to begin the film, we had only a few dozen people from our church and a handful of new visitors. Samuel felt we should begin right on time, but I told him to wait a few more minutes while I went outside onto the sidewalk to see if anyone else was coming. When I walked out from around the corner, a caravan of thirty to forty kids came walking up the block, heading our way. There were two adults with them, and as I looked at their costumes, I concluded that those kids had been trick-or-treating together, probably coming from the same block or the same housing project.

I smiled real big at the chaperones and told them (loud enough for all the kids to hear) that we'd love for their group to come to our free movie and have all the popcorn and candy they could eat, and then they could carry home with them any leftover candy. All the kids started cheering and jumping for joy, and the chaperones looked at each other, wondering what to do. How could they say no? It might cause a riot behind them.

"But they're dressed up as witches and goblins and ghosts," one of the chaperones objected. "You sure you want them to come into your church dressed like that?"

"No problem," I said as I opened the front door and escorted them all in, realizing if I asked them to go home and change, we'd surely never see them again. They loved the movie, and we all had a great time, except for some of our regulars who often came up from the mother church to help. They abruptly and angrily left at the end of the movie.

Early Monday morning, Pastor Dave's secretary called me and said he'd like for me to come to the Tuesday staff meeting a half hour early to speak with him. I spent much of Monday and Tuesday morning wondering what Pastor Dave would want to discuss with me and why it was so urgent that it required a definite appointment. As I nervously made my way into his office and sat down, I noticed he had a puzzled and stern look on his face. He said, "Charles, you're like a son to me so I'm going to speak frankly with you. Do you feel that we as leaders in the church should try to become like the world in order to reach the world?"

"No, sir."

"Wouldn't you agree that Halloween is a very demonic holiday that we Christians should have nothing to do with?"

"Yes, I agree," I answered.

"Then why did you have a costume party at your church on Halloween night?"

"What? Oh...yeah. Well, we didn't plan it that way. It was scheduled as a free movie night." I then explained that when I saw the kids coming around the corner, I knew the only way to get them to come was to allow them to come "just as they were."

Pastor Dave let out a long and hearty laugh and said, "My, that's exactly what I would have done! A few of your members told me you had a Halloween costume party!"

"Actually, Pastor Dave, if they had stayed around to help us clean up the huge mess, they would have heard me address the congregation as to what happened and why."

After a year and a half of ministering almost non-stop, my health began to break down. Pastor Dave's bright and caring secretary noticed my deep cough and asked how long had it been since I had had a vacation.

"I don't remember," I said.

"When's the last time you had a full week off?"

"Since before I started in the Bronx. It seems a crisis in someone's family occurs every week." (It didn't help that I didn't have a wife to encourage me to slow down.)

"That's what we thought. Pastor Dave would like to send you to Texas for a week for some rest. I'll buy your ticket today and you can plan on being gone from next Monday to the following Monday. OK?"

"OK. Thank you."

Pastor Dave's World Challenge headquarters, located in Lindale, Texas, was a modest office with a warehouse attached and a small guesthouse located behind it. As I made plans to visit there, I thought about how Lindale must have been quite the place to be in the 1980s—a small east Texas town filled with genuine world changers. Leonard Ravenhill, author of the classic *Why Revival Tarries* and mentor to Pastor Dave, lived there. Down the street was one of the best Christian singing groups in the nation, the 2nd Chapter of Acts. Keith and Melody Green moved their Last Days Ministries there, and Winkie Pratney's ministry was also located nearby. I was told that Pastor Dave, who hated flying, chose Lindale as his headquarters because it's in the central part of the United States, making any domestic trip doable by way of car or bus.

Leonard Ravenhill seemed to know how life altering it would be when he handed Brother Dave the Puritan classic *The Christian in Complete Armour,* saying to him, "This book is going to revolutionize your life. It has had a profound effect on my life, and I believe you are prepared to receive its message now." Pastor Dave was quoted as saying, "At first I put the book aside; it was too long, too wordy. Out of curiosity, I later scanned the first twenty-five pages. That is all it took to bring me to my knees. Gurnall, the pious Puritan, had touched something deep within me. His were such probing, scorching, searing words that they shook my inner man. I devoured the book with great zeal. I will forever bless the day it was placed in my hands."

That book caused Pastor Dave to cut back on his evangelistic crusades and return with renewed passion and fervency to his prayer closet. And one day he reappeared in public ministry with a burning message on his heart entitled "Holy Ground." After that, he went to New York for a series of meetings, and it was then that the Lord spoke to him about returning to the Big Apple to raise up a church in the Times Square section of Manhattan.

The only one that I knew for sure still living in Lindale was Leonard Ravenhill. Perhaps I could meet him while I was there. As soon as I arrived and unloaded my things in the guesthouse, I crashed into bed and spent the rest of the day there. I got up coughing the next day and did nothing more than take naps all day long. I didn't realize how worn out I'd gotten. On the seventh day of my eight-day vacation, I ventured out to Lindale to a restaurant. On the way back, I stopped at a pay phone and called Brother Ravenhill. I told him who I was, and that I worked with Pastor Dave, and that I was staying in his cottage behind his ministry building. I asked if I could come by and pray with him, but he said he was booked up solid. I told him I'd be leaving about noon tomorrow so maybe I could meet him the next time I came down. I was pretty bummed out about this because I really wanted to meet him. He was very kind to me over the telephone and said he was sorry and hung up. Well, at least I got to speak with him over the phone.

At 9:05 the following morning, one of the guys from the World Challenge office came knocking on the front door of the cottage.

"Hey Charles, Leonard Ravenhill just called and said that his nine o'clock appointment canceled and he'd like to meet with you now, if you're still available."

"You bet I am," I yelled back as I grabbed my sweater and the keys to the ministry van. "Please call him back and tell him I'm on my way."

When I arrived, I seemed to walk into the home of the prime minister of England. His British accent, British décor, and British tea and shortbread made me feel like royalty. He told me that a pastor from Sydney, Australia, had scheduled a 9:00 A.M. meeting, but his flight was delayed because of storms near the Dallas airport. He said that the president of a Bible college was coming at 10:00, and then the leader of a denomination was scheduled for 11:00 A.M.

"Is it like this every day?" I asked. "People coming to see you from all over the world?"

"Only Mondays through Fridays. I don't schedule any appointments on the weekends."

I noticed the time was 9:25 so I said, "Brother Ravenhill, even more than talking with you, I'd love to pray with you."

Boy, he sure liked that idea! "Splendid," he said, and we prayed together about everything in our lives, especially for Pastor Dave and Gwen and their kids, my family, Times Square Church, the Bronx, New York City, our country, our president, and other political leaders. The ring of the doorbell soon interrupted our prayers, and we both stopped and listened as his wife greeted the Bible college president and ushered him into the adjacent room.

"Well, Charles, it's almost ten o'clock and time for my next visitor," he said as he slowly stood up. "It's been great meeting you and praying with you. Most of my visitors want to talk and ask questions and get some advice from this old man. But I, like you, would rather pray than talk. Here's a book on prayer that I'll sign and give to you as a gift. You remind me of a dear pastor I know in Canada named Carter Conlon. He prays for hours every day. A real touch of God on his life."

"Brother Ravenhill, before I go, there actually is one question that I've been dying to ask you."

"OK. What is it?"

"Do you think America will experience one last true revival before the end?"

"Of course!" he said without hesitation.

"But how can you be so sure?"

He looked at his watch and said, "How many people in this town do you think got up and prayed before they went to work today?"

"Oh, probably a handful, I guess."

"And how many of those spent quality, heartfelt time with their Lord?"

"Probably not very many of them."

"Well, does that sound to you like His wife has made herself ready for the marriage?" I shook my head no and realized he was referring to the verse in Revelation that says:

> *Let us be glad and rejoice and give Him glory, for the marriage of the Lamb has come, and His wife has made herself ready* (Revelation 19:7).

I thanked him, took the book in one hand, vigorously shook his other hand, and left. Brother Ravenhill's comments gave me a lot of hope that the Church will become revived and passionate about her Groom in the years to come. For those who have never been blessed by Brother Ravenhill's sermons or books (which I encourage you to listen to and read), here are some of my favorite quotes of his regarding prayer, the Church, revival, and holiness:

> "How do you learn to pray? Well, how do you learn to swim? Do you sit in a chair with your feet up, drinking coke, learning to swim? No, you get down and you struggle. That's how you learn to pray."

> "No man is greater than his prayer life. If you tell me this, I'll tell you how spiritual you are: will you tell me how much you pray?"

> "This generation of Christians is responsible for this generation of lost souls!"

"You never have to advertise a fire. Everyone comes running when there's a fire. Likewise, if your church is on fire, you will not have to advertise it. The community will already know it."

"I want to see the glory of God come among us so that our young people don't have to be told to go to church but instead will long to get to the sanctuary where God is."

"To graduate a preacher from a seminary without a prayer life is like sending a car from the assembly line without a motor."

"The king in America—[you say] there isn't one. Yes there is, his name is King Sport and his wife is Queen Entertainment. The devil's substitute for joy is entertainment. Where there is no joy, you have to fill it up with entertainment. The more joy you have in God, the less entertainment you need outside of yourself."

8

"It's the backbone of Times Square Church."

WHEN I RETURNED TO THE BRONX, THE CYCLE OF OVERWORKING AND under-resting began all over again. A case of bronchitis set in that I simply could not shake. I tried fasting and praying and standing on the Word and going to healing services. Nothing helped. I then tried a routine of strong antibiotics prescribed by a local physician, and then another round of even stronger antibiotics. Still no improvement. A friend named Arnie, a member of Times Square Church who would eventually move to Israel as a missionary, came to visit me in the Bronx.

"Charles, are you sure you have bronchitis?"

"That's what the doctors say I have!"

"Well, for years my wife was misdiagnosed, and when we finally found out what she really had, the right medicine cleared it up in a few weeks."

"How did you find that out?"

"By going to one of the best doctors in Manhattan, a diagnostic expert named Dr. Boxhill. His office is on Central Park West, but he's not cheap."

"I don't know," I slowly replied.

"Charles, he's a genius, and he's worth it. He doesn't take any insurance and he charges 250 dollars a visit. Please, Charles, go to him," Arnie insisted as he handed me his contact information and a wad of twenty-dollar bills, totaling 260 dollars.

"OK. I'll go."

I could tell right away how brilliant Dr. Boxhill was, not just because of the many degrees on his wall, but also because of the way he asked probing questions that no one else had ever bothered to ask me.

"It looks like you have the Epstein-Barr virus."

"What is *that?*" I asked in shock.

"Well, it's also called the yuppie disease or mononucleosis."

"How did I get it?"

"Probably by working too hard. I won't know for sure until the test results come back, but I'm 99 percent sure that's what you have. I need to warn you...in three days you will be almost too weak to stand. You'll need complete bed rest for a month, and then it will take six to nine months to recover, if you ever do fully recover. Mr. Simpson, if you don't stop and get some bed rest, you're an inch away from getting tuberculosis. I highly recommend you take my advice."

I headed directly to Pastor Dave's office, which at the time was only a few blocks south and three blocks west of the doctor's office. I told him exactly what the doctor said and concluded (with tears in my eyes), "I guess I need to find someone I can hand the South Bronx Church over to."

"Charles, don't ever make major decisions when you're sick, depressed, or worn out, which pretty much describes your condition right now. Why don't we fly you down to Tennessee and you can stay with your mom in Cleveland for a month or two? I can get some of our team to take over the work in the Bronx in the meantime."

I nodded my head in agreement, silently wondering why the Lord hadn't just healed me already, as I lowered my shame-filled eyes down to my feet.

In order to help me shake off the condemnation I felt over my predicament, Pastor Dave smiled and said, "Well, I guess you're walking in my footsteps, for sure." I looked up with bewilderment on my face as he continued: "When I first came to this city, I burned myself out trying to fix all the problems I saw. I became worn out and ended up getting mononucleosis. I had to be hospitalized for six weeks, and even then it took me a while to recover. I know how needy the South Bronx is. The need can indicate a call, but it is not to dictate the call."

"Can you explain that a bit further, Pastor Dave?"

"Sure. OK, you're called to start and pastor a church in the Bronx. But every need you see is not yours to try to fulfill. When did the prodigal son come to himself?"

"I guess when he was feeding the pigs?"

"The verse right before *'And he came to himself'* says, *'no man gave to him.'* The prodigal son found himself in a place where no one helped him so he would look up to Heaven for help. We need to differentiate between our calling and the needs of the people around us. And no one is able to meet every need he sees. This needy city causes the best of us to overdo it, along with other impure motives that the Lord has to deal with us about."

Three long days later, I walked from my old bedroom in Mom's house in Cleveland, Tennessee, to go brush my teeth in the bathroom sink. I blacked out and fainted and somehow fell against the corner of the room, sliding down until I was sitting on top of the bathroom trashcan. I finally woke up, perhaps hours later, finding that I'd been thrown away!

"Well, Lord, why don't You just dispose of me," I joked out loud as I pried myself off the trashcan. "Maybe I should go toss myself headfirst into the large garbage can out in the backyard!"

Just as the doctor predicted, I could hardly move for the next month. I spent almost the entire time lying in bed, thinking and praying. I thought about the last service we had in the Bronx when my leadership team gathered around me and fervently prayed, once again, that I would be supernaturally healed so I wouldn't have to take an untimely sabbatical. I thought about the guest speaker we had that day, the director of Teen Challenge in Ireland. When he prayed over me, he quoted the verse *"...Well done, good and faithful servant; you have been faithful over a few things, I will make you ruler over many things..."* (Matt. 25:23). What could that possibly mean? Was my time in the Bronx over? Where would I go if it was?

I faced the fact that one of the reasons why I worked too hard was that I was somehow trying to earn God's smile by my efforts. I read in the Scriptures that Jesus had His Father's approval and affirmation even before His ministry began. At His baptism, the Father audibly declared from Heaven, *"You are My beloved Son, in whom I am well pleased"* (Mark 1:11; Matt. 3:17). Ministry should come from an over-flow of gratitude for what Jesus has done for me instead of being a way to somehow prove to Him how hard I can work for God. I also saw that I worked too hard at trying to follow in the steps of Pastor Dave by building a Times Square Church in the Bronx. I realized that although we are all to follow in the faith-filled steps of Abraham, this does not mean that we must move to Canaan and become wandering patriarchs! I let the Lord deal with my motives, surrendered my life to Him afresh, and I heard His gentle whisper that my assignment in the Bronx was over. Then, quite suddenly, I was completely healed. My strength returned 100 percent. Praise God!

I flew back to New York and told Pastor Dave that I let the Lord deal with the roots of my workaholism and that God had spoken to me. My time in the Bronx was over, and I was completely well. My team in the Bronx told me they'd heard rumors that Brooklyn Tab- ernacle was considering planting a sister church in the South Bronx. Pastor Dave and Pastor Cymbala soon discussed the situation. The couple that was ready to plant the new church was willing to take over South Bronx Church, renaming it South Bronx Tabernacle. I then asked Pastor Dave if I could move back into my old cubbyhole room in the theater for a few months, or at least until I knew what my next assignment was. He was more than happy to consent. My congregation in the Bronx was perplexed that I left them without knowing what my next step was, and frankly, so was I.

A few weeks later, Pastor Dave came over to the church and asked one of the workers to let me know that he wanted to speak with me and would be waiting on the stage in the chair in which he sat during services. I quickly made my way down to the stage and joined him. "Charles, all of us pastors have been praying a lot for you."

"Thank you so much," I replied with sincere gratitude.

"And we all agree that we would like for you to come on the pas- toral staff here as an associate pastor, as the pastor of prayer."

"What?" I responded in total bewilderment. "But what about what happened in the South Bronx? I failed in the Bronx. I got too sick to continue. Why would you want to hire a failure?"

"You didn't fail in the Bronx! You didn't choose to get so sick that you had to step down! You worked hard in an impoverished neighborhood for two full years. You established a congregation and faithfully ministered God's Word there." By this time, he was almost yelling. "That's not failure!" he exclaimed. I realized he was attack- ing the lies of the enemy and not attacking me personally. But I was still shocked, and I just stared at him as he waited for me to reply. He probably expected me to jump at the golden opportunity because when I gave him my answer, surprise then filled his face.

I said to him, "Pastor Dave, I'm honored, but I'll have to pray about this." We both stood up at the same time and quickly

97

walked away, he to the office across the street and I back to my cubbyhole room.

Sometimes when Christians respond by saying, "I'll pray about it," it's nothing more than a polite, "No, thanks." But I meant it. I went to my little room and stayed on my knees for a long time, travailing in prayer. And the more I prayed, the more peace I felt. Then I felt tremendous joy—joy unspeakable and full of glory. I got up, walked over to my bookshelf, and randomly pulled a book off the shelf. I picked out one that I hadn't begun reading yet. It was the book *Revival God's Way* by Leonard Ravenhill. I opened it up in the middle, looked down, and read aloud:

> Without exception, all true revivals of the past began after years of agonizing, hell-robbing, earthshaking, Heaven-sent intercession. The secret to true revival in our own day is still the same. But where, oh where, are the intercessors? Some of us older souls remember when whole nights were given to prayer in the church. There are churches with a Senior Pastor, Associate Pastor, Music Pastor, or Youth Pastor, but where, oh where, is there a church with a Pastor of Prayer?[19]

I was trembling with excitement. I literally ran across the street and into Pastor Dave's office unannounced. (Never did that before, but I felt like a kid who had to share with his daddy right away. I just couldn't help myself.) "Pastor Dave, Pastor Dave, the answer's yes! Yes, I'll be the pastor of prayer. The more I prayed about it, the more peace I felt. And then I pulled out this Ravenhill book and opened it up right to this page! Look at what it says!"

Pastor Dave read it out loud, laughed, and then carefully read it again to himself. "Charles, that's great! Let's start a Thursday night prayer meeting next week! Here's a booklet I found in an old bookstore I want you to have. I think it's out of print so don't lose it." I looked down and read the title to myself: *Daniel Nash, Prevailing*

Prince of Prayer. A congregation Daniel Nash deeply loved had voted him out of the pastorate. Soon afterward, he had a serious illness called inflamed eyes. For several weeks he had to be kept in a dark room, where he gave himself to prayer. He then began one of the greatest ministries of prayer evangelism recorded in history. He went out ahead of the revivalist Charles Finney and prayed down God's blessings and power on his evangelistic efforts.

When I had been pastoring in the Bronx, many of those who helped me would also attend the Sunday evening services at Times Square Church. I was told over and over that my sermons in the afternoon were the same messages Pastor Dave preached later in the evening. When I began attending Sunday nights, amazingly two out of three times it would be the same message, with the same Scripture passages! Talk about a confidence booster! So I was excited and ready when Pastor Dave said the format of the Thursday evening services should include some worship, a twenty-minute sermon on prayer, and then intercession as the Spirit of God led.

He opened and led the first Thursday evening prayer service, and at the end, he introduced me as the new pastor of prayer and the one who would be leading those meetings from then on. They took place in the main sanctuary with the maroon stage curtain closed. I would stand in the middle of the altar and lead us in songs that everyone knew and then preach my heart out on prayer for twenty minutes. And then we prayed—really prayed. During the fourth or fifth prayer service, I was not aware that Pastor Dave was sitting in his seat on the stage behind the curtain, quietly listening to the service.

Right as I ended my little sermon, Pastor Dave got so excited that he came out from behind the curtain and told the surprised crowd, "Folks, what Pastor Charles just shared with you is exactly what God has been speaking to me all day long. It's the Lord!"

A few weeks later, the very same thing happened, but even more dramatically. Pastor Dave came out, saying to the hundreds of people gathered there that my twenty-minute sermon was exactly what he was preaching the following Sunday. Same verses, same context. Those prayer meetings became, in Pastor Dave's words, "the backbone of Times Square Church." The very week they started, everyone noticed a difference as we experienced more of God's presence, peace, and power in all the church services.

One Thursday afternoon while I was preparing for the evening prayer meeting, I heard the Lord speaking to me about taking authority. I guess I needed to teach on authority in prayer. God said to my waiting heart, "Not only are you to teach it; you need to put it into practice. When someone tries to disrupt the service this evening, rebuke him in My name and everything will be OK." All afternoon I wondered how this warning would play out: Would radical Muslims or angry activists try to disrupt the service, like they sometimes did on Sundays? Everything seemed to be going smoothly for the first part of the service. I led the group of about three hundred faithful intercessors in a few well-known and simple choruses and then preached for about twenty minutes on how we have been given Jesus's name and the authority of His name to use in our prayers. I was about to invite everyone to the front to call on the Lord together for the next hour. Suddenly, a strange-looking chubby man with a suitcase came walking, almost running, down one of the church's aisles, heading straight toward me.

He yelled out, "I have a bomb, and I'm going to blow this place to pieces!"

Because of the earlier warning from the Holy Spirit, I was ready. I walked right up to that Goliath and said, "In the authority of Jesus's name, I command you to turn around right now and walk out of here!" The man stopped, turned completely around, and obediently walked out of the church as though he had no choice in the matter—which he didn't!

The congregation sat there shocked and then amazed at what had unfolded. I went right along with the meeting, not missing a beat. It wasn't until I woke up the next morning that I thought, "Oh my! What if that suitcase really did have a bomb in it? It might have even been a dirty nuclear bomb!"

I read that Charles Spurgeon attributed the ten-year revival that his church in London experienced to the prayer meetings that took place in its basement during the services. How cool was that! We could do that! Soon a room opened up in the basement, directly underneath the main sanctuary, and we developed prayer teams to intercede for the people sitting in the seats directly above us. We worshiped in the main sanctuary, and then when the children were released to go to children's church before the sermon began, we went down to the prayer room. We all noticed another increase of God's presence as soon as those prayer meetings started. I taught the teams that our prayer time in that room was not for Aunt Sue or the people in China but specifically for the people attending the service right at that moment. The room could only hold about twenty people so we had a sign-up sheet that filled up a half hour before the services began!

We then started having prayer at the altar before each service. People came thirty to forty-five minutes early anyway (to get a good seat) so we decided that we might as well make use of that time. Hundreds of people joined me as we gathered up front and called upon God for His blessings on the service. We then started noonday prayer meetings for those who worked in the area. My life felt like one continuous, glorious prayer meeting!

9

"This could destroy the calling on your life."

WHILE LIVING AND PASTORING IN THE BRONX, THERE WAS A SISTER IN MY church I thought God was bringing my way to be my wife, but I was very wrong. One of the pastors at Brooklyn Tabernacle warned me that this particular sister had been in a mental hospital and was still not in her right mind and was not being honest with me. She didn't tell me she had moved in (for a season) with one of the male doctors who were treating her. When I came on staff at Times Square Church as the pastor of prayer, Pastor Dave told me, "Charles, if you don't hear clearly from the Lord whom to marry, this could destroy the calling on your life."

One Sunday evening, Pastor Dave preached on our need to learn how to patiently wait on the Lord and sit in His presence. After the altar call was given and people went back to their seats, the presence of God was so strong that no one wanted to leave. I doubt if more than 20 people out of the capacity crowd of 1,500 got up and left. The choir sang another song, and another, and another. After the sixth extra song, Pastor Dave got up and addressed the congregation.

"Beloved, there are times when staying in God's presence is more important than getting enough sleep, getting enough to eat, or getting enough of anything else. I need more of God so I'm going to sing to the Lord some more, and I encourage you to stay as long as God's overwhelming presence stays upon this service."

He sat down and we sang many more songs as the glory of the Lord filled the place. I will never forget that meeting. I stayed until the end of the very last song, partly because I lived in the back of the building! As the time approached 2:00 A.M. and I was peacefully floating to my room, I recalled Pastor Gary asking me to consider joining him on a mission trip to Poland and Romania that he was about to take. How I'd love to go with him. "Lord," I said, with my spirits high and my faith soaring, "so many times in Your Word You spoke through dreams. Speak to me tonight in a dream."[20] I was hoping and expecting the Lord to give me a dream about going with Gary, or about not going with him, so I could give him a definite answer.

I awoke in the middle of the night, my room pitch black except for the red numbers on my clock radio. Three thirty-three, it read. I suddenly recalled the vivid dream I just had. It was about one of the sisters who often prayed beside me during our pre-service prayer meetings at the altar. In the dream, she and I were on our knees together in a living room, praying as husband and wife. "Oh, no. I think that sister's married," I said to myself. (She didn't have that look across her face that so many Christian sisters have, the look that screams, "I'm single and available and desperate!") No, she had the contented look of a happily married wife. "Lord, if this is an attack from the enemy, I'll have nothing of it." I turned on the bright overhead light and got out of bed and paced back and forth for the next hour, fervently praying against any attack from a spirit of adultery.

Suddenly, the same overwhelming presence from the service the night before invaded my little room. As the presence of God filled the place, I got on my knees in reverence and recalled a bit of advice

Pastor Dave gave me one time: "Trust what you hear when you're in God's presence. Doubt what you hear when your heart is filled with fears and anxieties." I quieted my soul and asked, "Lord, what is it?"

"Charles, this woman you dreamt about is going to be your wife. I'm going to tell you about her so you will know this is of Me. She's in her mid-twenties and was saved in a Pentecostal church." And then the presence lifted and I crawled back into bed.

At the Tuesday evening prayer meeting before the service, she was praying right beside me, along with hundreds of others who gathered at the front to pray. As the maroon curtain rose (signaling it was time to begin), we intercessors went back to our saved seats, mine being on the platform right behind Pastor Dave. I asked a sister on the way back, "Did you see the sister who was praying next to me tonight?"

"Yeah," she said with a snicker. "Why do you ask?"

"What's her name?"

"That's Lynn."

"Do you know how old she is?"

She smiled real big and said, "No, but I know someone who would know. You know Lois, the usher over there? You can ask her about Lynn. They're friends."

"Thanks," I said as I hurried to the platform. Lois was ushering the aisle closest to the platform entrance. When I made my way down to the prayer room when the kids were dismissed, I stopped and said, "Hi, Lois. Can I talk with you for a moment after the service?"

"Sure, but um..."

"I gotta go to the prayer room. See you after the service." I knew she wanted to ask what I'd like to talk about, and I hated to keep her hanging, but it would have to wait.

There was a long line of people waiting to see me after the service for various reasons. I was also in charge of hospital visitation and the AIDS ministry so I was always flooded with people requesting that I (or someone from my trained volunteer team) would visit their relatives in need. Finally, Lois was escorted back behind the stage where we pastors briefly spoke with people. (If conversations needed to be longer, we'd make appointments for them to see us across the street another day at the 38th-floor church offices.)

"Hi, Lois. Let's go over to that bench and sit for a minute." She seemed quite nervous, and there were still at least ten people waiting to see me so I decided to get right to the point.

"You know the sister who often prays right next to me at the altar?"

"Yes, Lynn. She's a good friend of mine."

"Was she saved in a Pentecostal church?"

"Yes, in a Pentecostal church on the Lower East Side."

"Is she in her mid-twenties?"

"Yes, she's twenty-four, almost twenty-five. Hey, wait a minute. How do you know this, and why are you asking me about her?"

"Well, I had a dream about her, and we..."

"Oh my!" she nearly screamed. "She's going to be your wife!"

"Shhhh!" I said. "If this is of God, it will work itself out."

"Oh, this is awesome," Lois said as she took out a fan and started fanning herself as if she didn't hear a word I just said.

"Lois, if this is of God, it will work out. But I need you to promise me that you won't say a word to anyone. OK?"

"OK! OK!" she eagerly said as though I had just asked if she'd like to be a part of the wedding party. I could see her mind was wandering off in a million directions.

"Not a word to anyone. Right?"

"Right," and she left, still fanning herself as she hurried out. Little did I know that Lynn was Lois's best friend, and Lynn was waiting for her to come out from behind the stage. They waited until they were out of the church to begin speaking.

"So, what did Pastor Charles have to tell you? Did he give you a prophetic word?"

"Lynn, you know I tell you everything, but I can't tell you this. I promised Pastor Charles I wouldn't say anything to you...I mean, that I wouldn't say anything."

"What! Lois, please tell me yes or no. Does this have to do with you or me?"

No response.

"Does this have to do with my going back to school?"

"You could say that!"

"Does this have to do with my going into ministry?"

"You certainly could say that!"

"Lois, what in the world is this about?"

"Lynn, all I can tell you is you'd better pray like you've never prayed in your life!"

"What?" Lynn exclaimed as she stopped in her tracks.

"Lynn, Pastor Charles saw you in a dream. And then the Lord told him all about you. You're going to be his wife!"

"What! Be his wife!" Lynn gasped. "What if he's missing it?"

Lois looked around to see if anyone was snooping and then said, "Missing it? If the pastor of prayer of Times Square Church is missing it, I will never come back here again. I'll start Lois Tabernacle in my living room and you can join me. OK?" Lynn headed to her bus, dazed and shocked.

Neither Lois nor Lynn attended the next Thursday or Friday evening service, or the Sunday morning service. Maybe they'd never come back! Sunday evening, about an hour after the service was over, the head usher said to me, "Pastor Charles, there are two more people in line to speak with you...no, make that three," as Lois stepped into the line.

She had such a horrible look on her face that I thought of all kinds of negative scenarios about the need for a hospital visit to one of her family members.

"Pastor Charles," she mumbled with her head down, not giving me any eye contact whatsoever. "I'm so sorry."

"Sorry about what?" I said with a little anger and a lot of anxiety.

"Well, Lynn is my best friend, more like a daughter to me."

"You didn't tell her, did you?"

She nodded her head up and down.

"Oh no," I said. I got up and walked away as Pastor Dave's words rang in my ears: "If you don't hear clearly from the Lord whom to marry, this could destroy the calling on your life."

I went up to my room, but I couldn't sleep. "Lord, I'm really in turmoil. I didn't think Lois would tell anyone, much less Lynn. She gave me her word. I don't know what to do. I'm really good at guessing people's ages. Maybe I just happened to guess that she was saved in a Pentecostal church."

At about five in the morning, sleep still hadn't come to me. I almost dozed off about ten times, but each time I thought about Pastor Dave's warning and how shocked Lynn must be, and how good I am at guessing people's ages, and how much responsibility I had as an associate pastor to set a good example. I couldn't even seem to pray through, I guess because my prayers were so mixed with such apprehension. I recalled one of Pastor Dave's sermons and decided it was time to put his words into practice. I would forget about all my problems for a while and simply worship the Lord. I put on a worship tape and began to sing along with it. After a while, the cassette clicked off, and I kept singing. The presence of God came upon me really strong.

"Charles," I heard the Lord say within my heart, "Lynn is going to be your wife. I want you to know this and I want you to be certain about it so I'm going to tell you something about her that you could never guess, so you will know this is of Me. Her parents were separated when she was very young, and yet they are still in court over it."

I could hardly wait until the Tuesday night service. But no Lois, and no Lynn. Neither were they at the Thursday or Friday services. Finally, I saw them walking into the Sunday morning service together, right as the worship began. I then noticed they were lingering together in the main lobby afterward so I took a deep breath and made my way over to them. "Wow, Lynn is really pretty," I thought to myself as I approached them.

"Hi, Lois and Lynn. Would you two like to go with me to Applejack Diner and get some lunch?"

They looked at each other and then at me, and Lois said, "OK." Lynn didn't say a single word. I guess she didn't know what to say. Lois didn't know how to stop talking. I guess it was nervous talk. She talked as we waited for a table, as we waited for our food, as we finished our meal. Finally, she said, "I need to use the restroom. Be right back."

Finally, Lynn and I were alone. I just had to ask her. "So, tell me about your parents."

"Well, it's surely a strange thing. My parents separated when I was two, and yet they're still in court over alimony and...whatever." She kept talking, but I couldn't hear her. It took all my energy to refrain myself from dropping my dessert spoon and saying, "You're going to be my wife!" From that moment on, and to this day, there's never been an inkling of a doubt that the Lord supernaturally brought us together. All the travailing in prayer about this was surely worth it!

As we exited the diner, Lois suddenly decided to walk home alone in order to give us some time together. I said to Lynn, "You know, dreams and visions and things like that are fine, but if it's OK with you, I'd like to put all that stuff behind us and just be friends. OK?"

She breathed out a huge sigh of relief and said, "OK! I'll walk you back to the church and then I'll take the bus home to my mom's in Washington Heights." On the way back, I found out that she was a schoolteacher and had off the entire month ahead.

"Lynn, would you like to come down to the church sometime and pray with me?"

"OK. I can come down the day after tomorrow."

From that day on, we spent the next fifty consecutive days together, primarily eating at one of the many Theater District restaurants after spending time praying together. There was an open room directly under the stage where altar counseling took place. Workers often walked through the area during the day, so it was semi-private but not too private as to be indiscreet. As we prayed there daily together (she too is an intercessor), God knit our hearts together and we fell in love with each other. And then I told her all about the dream and the words the Lord told me about her.

One day, Pastor Dave said to me with a big fatherly smile, "Charles, the church cleaning staff tells me that you're always praying with a certain girl under the stage in the counseling area."

"Yes. Her name is Lynn."

"I'd like to meet her tonight, after the evening service."

"Sure."

At the end of the Sunday evening service, one of the ushers escorted Lynn to the back and she stood beside me as we waited for Pastor Dave to finish greeting folks from another country. His wife, Gwen, was with him backstage. Finally, the visitors said goodbye, and Pastor Dave and his wife walked over to us.

"Pastor Dave and Gwen, this is Lynn."

"Charles," Pastor Dave said as he stared at Lynn, "I've always been very frank and open with you, and I just want to say...this is

God! This is God!" Pastor Dave looked deeply into Lynn's eyes and said, "I see Jesus in you. Thank You, Lord, for having Your way in her life."

Sister Gwen then hugged Lynn and said, "Welcome to the inner circle, honey. I'm sure we're going to love you as much as we love Charles." We'll never forget that truly precious moment.

The following Tuesday, I was sitting in Pastor Dave's office sharing with Barbara, his secretary, everything I knew about Lynn. We were waiting for Pastor Dave to finish up a meeting with his son-in-law, Roger, the church treasurer. When he sat down next to me, he got right to the point. "Charles, I don't believe in long marriage engagements. When you know it's God, why wait? Waiting too long just puts you in hard situations. Would you and Lynn like to get married soon?"

"Well, I didn't want to get engaged until you met her. So, we just got engaged, and it's the middle of October. We did talk about how nice it would be to have a Christmas wedding. Manhattan is such an awesome place during the holidays."

"Perfect. Let's have a Christmas wedding!"

A few weeks before the wedding, Pastor Dave asked Lynn and me to walk with him to his apartment at the Worldwide Plaza after a Sunday evening service.

"So, how did your marriage counseling session go with Pastor Bob?" he asked us as we walked together.

"It was great. He and I exchanged amazing stories about how the Lord brought our wives to us," I replied.

"Yeah. I'm not so good with counseling. Not like you, Charles. I get impatient hearing people's long stories. I like to get to the point. For instance, here's my advice to you both." He stopped and faced us as though we were his little congregation, and then came the sermonette. He said, "Have a lot of mercy on each other, especially in the first year. When you have disputes, just say, 'I'll have mercy on you if you'll have mercy on me!'" Lynn and I laughed because it sounded so silly and so simplistic. He then continued, "Especially after the first year, you two are going to have such a wonderful life together. It's gonna be like Heaven on earth." His little bit of advice did go a long way toward making our first year smooth, and his prophetic word continues to come to pass. Thank God!

We continued walking to the Worldwide Plaza with him. When he got into the elevator, instead of saying, "See you later," he said, "Step in, and come with me." He pushed B instead of 34, and we headed down to the basement. As we walked over to his wife's almost brand-new Honda Accord, he pulled the keys out of his pocket and said, "My wife doesn't like driving in the city. We'd like to give this car to you and Lynn as an early wedding gift. Besides, with all the hospitals you visit each week, you need a dependable car. As a matter of fact, Charles, your plate is so full. If Lynn would be willing to quit her teaching job and be your full-time secretary, we'll double your salary."

We were so overwhelmed with his generosity, all we knew to do was to cry and nod our heads in thanks and agreement.

"It's yours. You can give Lynn a ride home if you'd like."

As we drove out of the underground lot, Lynn said, "What a blessing it must be to be so well-off financially that you can give so generously. Did you see how much joy it gave Pastor Dave to give us this nice car? I'd like to be able to bless people like that one day." I drove her home to her mom's in Washington Heights and then drove back to the Worldwide Plaza parking lot.

A few weeks before our wedding, I realized that even with the money Lynn had saved up while working for the Board of Education and living at home with her mom, it would be hard to get enough furniture for our new apartment. A friend in church named Vinny was looking for someone to help him with a big painting job in New Jersey.

"Lynn, I think I'm gonna help Vinny paint that house on Monday and Tuesday. He'll give me two hundred dollars a day, and that's really good money. We need some extra money."

"Have you prayed about it?" she asked on the other end of the line, as I was talking to her from one of the church's old-fashioned phone booths behind the stage.

"No, but he starts tomorrow morning, and he needs the answer right now."

"I don't feel peace about it, Charles. I don't think you should do it. You're working hard enough, and we should trust God to bring in the extra money we need."

"I don't know," I said reluctantly.

I quickly ended the conversation as Vinny approached me, saying, "I gotta go, Charles. I start early tomorrow morning. Is it a yes or a no?"

"Yes, I'll help you. What's the train stop in Jersey where you'll pick me up?"

The next day, although I had stayed up late due to emergency counseling, I woke up at 4:00 A.M. I needed to leave by 5:00 in order to catch the 5:20 train so Vinny could pick me up at 7:05 somewhere in New Jersey. When I saw him drive into the train station parking lot a half hour late, I could tell something was wrong.

"Vinny, what's the matter?"

"Joe's wife called me this morning. She doesn't want the house painted."

"She can just back out of the agreement like that?"

"Joe died of a heart attack yesterday, Charles."

On the long train ride back to the city, I thought about how when Lynn and I get married, maybe I should listen to her, especially when she doesn't have peace about things!

At the Friday night service, right before our Saturday wedding, Pastor Dave got up and invited the entire church to the wedding ceremony. Maybe no one told him that the reception would be in the lower rotunda, which should only hold a hundred and not the hundreds who showed up. That would be the last wedding reception in the lower rotunda! Every Christmas a wealthy couple in the congregation purchased tons of red poinsettias, filling the stage with color and cheer. They decided to get them a couple days early, so they were in place for our December 22nd wedding.

Pastor Bob Phillips, also known as Marrying Bob, officiated the service. As he and I were waiting backstage, I looked out beyond the flowers and noticed that the lower level was packed with friends and family members. I saw my mom and Lynn's mom and my dear friend, Charles Thompson, who led me to the Lord so many years ago when I was a very lost teenager. I was trying real hard not to get too nervous so I struck up a conversation with Pastor Bob. "How many weddings have you done, Pastor Bob?"

"I don't know. I stopped counting after a few hundred."

"No way!" I exclaimed.

He humbly nodded his head. What a relief! At least he wouldn't be nervous. He could do this in his sleep. As he noticed the swelling crowd, he said something I didn't quite hear clearly. I thought he said to me, "This sure took a lot of sweat." Was he actually referring to how the rest of the pastoral staff must have prayed extremely hard for God to bless me with such a lovely bride as Lynn? But still, it sounded weird to me, so I asked, "Pastor Bob, what did you just say?"

"I said, this is surely the biggest one yet," referring to the number of people present. As Lynn walked down the long aisle, I was amazed at how good the Lord had been to me! It never even dawned on me that most, if not all, of the people attending would be giving us wedding gifts. After the wedding ceremony and reception were over,

John (the new caretaker of the building) said to me, "And what do we do with all the wedding gifts, Pastor Charles?"

"Uh, can you put them in your office until I get back?"

"That's where they are right now, but they can't stay there until you get back from your honeymoon!" The look on my face said, "And why not?"

"Come with me," John demanded as he darted to his office, dangling his keys as he went. By the time we arrived, he had selected the right key, and when he opened the door, wow! The office was filled almost to the ceiling with large stuffed black garbage bags!

"All these bags...are filled with wedding gifts?"

"Yep," John said, "and they can't stay here."

Right then, my friend Vinny popped his head in and said, "Pastor Charles, I'll take them over to your new apartment in my van."

"Thanks so much, Vinny. The super has an extra key."

And then John said, "Pastor Charles, take the bag that's on my desk if you can get to it. Yeah, that one." I lifted it up and noticed it wasn't too heavy and didn't seem more than halfway filled, unlike the rest of them.

"Those are the cards," John explained. "Take that one with you."

It wasn't until halfway through our honeymoon that I remembered that bag in the trunk of our Honda Accord. "Hey, Lynn, you want to look at the cards we got?" Oh my! It seemed like every single card had a twenty-, a fifty-, or a hundred-dollar bill in it. Since Pastor Dave invited the entire church the night before the wedding, many of the guests decided to give us cash. We counted the money, and it totaled more than six thousand dollars!

"I told you the Lord would meet our needs," Lynn announced triumphantly.

10

"Don't ever try to be anointed."

AS SOON AS WE RETURNED FROM OUR TWO-WEEK HONEYMOON ON THE shores of Narragansett, Rhode Island, I preached the Tuesday evening service at Times Square Church. People said it was the best message I'd ever preached. I guess I need more two-week vacations!

Pastor Dave came up to me afterward and said, "Wow, married life already has done you a lot of good. That was a great message!" The next time I preached, Pastor Dave lingered around longer than usual. The only ones left in the building with me were John, my patiently waiting wife, and Pastor Dave. "Charles," he began, "you're like a son to me. And I want to treat you like I would Gary or Greg. So can I have permission to share at the end of your sermons some ways that I feel you could improve them?"

"That would be awesome, Pastor Dave."

"One day, you'll be preaching in various places, and if you can work out your little quirks now, it'll make you that much more effective in the future."

"Thanks," I said to him with sincerity and gratitude. "Can we start now? I mean, any recommendations about tonight's message?"

"Yes. I want you to get the tape and listen to it and notice that you said, 'Amen?' way too many times." Sure enough, I counted twenty "amens" in my sermon and determined to no longer "amen" the congregation to death! If they don't want to amen the "amen-able" parts of my sermon, then I shouldn't force it.

The next time I preached, it was a searing message from Hosea regarding how God sees our idolatry as spiritual adultery against Him.[21] For the first time in my life, a number of people (mostly first-time visitors) approached me afterward and essentially said the same thing. "Here's my address," they would say as they handed me a business card or a piece of paper with their information scribbled on it. "If you ever put that sermon into book form, please let me know."

Pastor Dave said to me, "Are you ready for another tip?"

"Yes, sir!"

"No matter how strong an Old Testament prophet's message was, it always included words of hope and encouragement. So, we need to do the same. Have you ever noticed how Hosea's last chapter is one of the most encouraging passages in the whole Old Testament?"

The next time I got up to preach, I tried really hard not to say "amen" too many times. I also tried to add plenty of encouragement at the end of the message. I tried a little too hard and for a little too long. It was a good message, but it wasn't a home run like some of my sermons. I take preaching very seriously and try my best to bring a word from the Lord to the congregation. I was hoping that Pastor Dave would once again pinpoint where I needed correction.

"Charles," he slowly began, choosing his words carefully as we were both standing on the stage together, "don't ever try to be anointed. Just try to meet the needs of the people you're ministering to, and the Lord will anoint you to do that. The anointing is to meet people's needs and not for a show."

"Do you think I'm becoming showy?"

"No, I don't. I guess I was referring to myself, also. Have a seat," he said as he motioned to a chair behind me. He sat next to me and continued. "When I pastored in Pennsylvania, people would come from all over to watch as I would minister in words of knowledge and words of wisdom.[22] I could walk up and down the aisle of my crowded church, call people out, and read their mail. It was truly supernatural. One day, I left the parsonage after arguing with Gwen and I stepped into the pulpit to do my thing, and the Lord stopped me. He said to me, 'David, My gifts are given to meet people's needs, not to create a circus atmosphere. From now on, you will mainly use these gifts in private.' When the gifts stopped flowing, the crowds soon left. And then, years later, while walking the streets of Brooklyn late at night, those gifts began to flow again. I'd walk up to an addict and the Lord would give me insight into what was going on deep in their heart. Then, hopefully, I would lead him to Christ. Just last night I spoke to a man on the streets at 3:00 in the morning—an addict named Joey. I knew his addiction started a few weeks after his father suddenly died, and I told him so. I expect to see him down here at the altar soon. My point is, the anointing is given to enable us to meet the needs of other people. Just focus on feeding the people God's Word. Then the anointing of the Holy Spirit will be there to help you accomplish this."

I vigorously shook his hand, knowing that if I could firmly grasp all his suggestions, it would really help me grow as a faithful minister of God's Word.

As John was letting us out of the side entrance, Pastor Dave said, "Oh yes, one more thing. If you preach more than forty to forty-five minutes, you're going to lose the people. The fastest way to ruin a good sermon is to go a little too long. If you can't make your point in forty minutes, give it up!"

"Told you," Lynn quietly whispered to me.

Pastor Dave was probably concerned that he was giving me too much correction. He soon made sure that I knew how he felt about my preaching. While having lunch with our mutual friend, a businessman named Don, he said to him that I was his favorite preacher. That very evening, Don called and told me about his luncheon with Pastor Dave and what he said about my being his favorite.

The last tip I remember getting from Pastor Dave is the most piercing one of all. I was preaching a message about prayerlessness in the Church. I encouraged the lukewarm among us to stop making excuses and truly repent of having a wishy-washy, on-again, off-again prayer life and do something about it. "Don't just come up to the altar week after week and then go back to the same busy lifestyle that essentially crowds God out and pushes prayer out of your schedule. Do you think church attendance will make up for your lack of prayer?" I then exhorted the congregation rather loudly, "Do you think a Mafia hitman giving a portion of his earnings to the church makes up for his murders?!" You could have heard a pin drop on the floor. Looking back now, I see that the illustration was too intense and didn't really fit in a message geared toward encouraging people to pray more.

Afterward, Pastor Dave told me that once I was done with altar counseling, he'd be waiting for me in the green room in the back. I tried to finish as soon as I could so that I wouldn't keep him waiting for too long. About twenty minutes later, I made my way to the back room where Pastor Dave was sitting. "Charles, I think a father's ceiling should be his children's floor. I'd love to see you stand upon my shoulders and receive even greater blessings and revelations from God. That was some message you preached tonight. It actually reminded me...of me. In a good sense, and also in a not-so-good sense."

"What do you mean, Pastor Dave?" I remarked as I slowly sat down next to him.

"I just received a letter today in the mail from Leonard Ravenhill, my mentor. I'd like you to read it." He carefully handed it to me as though it were a valuable piece of jewelry. I slowly unfolded it and read:

> Dear Brother Dave,
>
> I have really enjoyed the cassette messages you recently sent to me, and I've listened to every single one of them. Finally, I'm hearing less of your own frustrations and more of the Lord's heart for His imperfect Church through your sermons. Keep up the good work!
>
> Blessings, Len

I carefully folded the letter and handed it back to him. "You've grown a lot in these years I've known you, Charles. Just be careful that you don't become just like me. Don't become overly frustrated with all the shortcomings of God's people."

As Lynn and I got in our car and silently drove through the city to our apartment in Queens, I recalled all the times I heard Pastor Dave use that word *frustrated*. On multiple occasions I heard him say, "I'm so frustrated with the Charismatic church in America. What are they thinking? Don't they have any fear of God in their hearts?"

One day, he came out of his office and joined the pastoral staff prayer meeting, saying, "I just got off the phone with the wife of a well-known minister. You all would know him if I said his name. He's hooked on pornography, and she doesn't know what to do. I'm so frustrated with situations like these." Another month would hardly go by before another wife or son or staff member of a world-famous Charismatic television or radio preacher would call Pastor Dave, desperately asking how to handle the secret sinful behavior of the so-called "mighty man of God." I personally observed Pastor Dave become a lightning rod for the relatives of well-known ministers. No wonder he got overly frustrated. Only Jesus can carry the burden of knowing all the junk that goes on behind the scenes in many of the major Christian ministries around the world.

Pastor Dave's younger son, Pastor Greg, who led the college and career ministry, asked me if I could fill in for him while he went on vacation. The Lord gave me a very strong message on making marriage and ministry an idol and how we can conquer those entrapments only by falling more deeply in love with Jesus. I tried to be very serious but at the same time not portray a God who is frustrated with our shortcomings. At the altar call, there was a literal explosion of repentance, with many dear young men and women profusely weeping their eyes out. Afterward, a deep sense of the presence of the Lord filled the room as the Lord confirmed His Word by giving everyone a taste of Heaven. In His presence there is fullness of joy![23] We all lingered in His presence for a long time, all the way into the early hours of the morning.

"Wow, Charles," Greg exclaimed after hearing the reports of the lives changed that night, "you really did an awesome job. It looks like I'll be moving to Dallas in a few months, and if I do, I sure hope you can take over this group. You have a lot to impart to them."

I talked it over with Lynn, and she reminded me of my already over-extended schedule. "How many prayer meetings a week are you in charge of? Twelve? You only have one day off, and you're so tired by then that you sleep half the day. And you want to do more?"

"I'm sure if I take that group, they'll get someone to take some of the things I'm doing now," I reasoned.

"Like when you started the hospital visitation ministry, someone was supposed to take the AIDS ministry from you. That was a year ago, and you're still waiting for that. I don't know, honey."

"Well, maybe I'll just discuss it with Pastor Dave and see what he thinks."

A few weeks later, Pastor Dave and I were together in his office. "Pastor Dave, what would you say if I was considering asking you if I could take over the college ministry when Greg leaves?"

"Are you not already too busy? Actually Charles, that brings up something that's been on my heart for a while. You're a pastor and not just an associate. I can't be selfish and hold on to you forever."

"Pastor Dave, I'll gladly be like a Daniel Nash to your Finney for the rest of my life. I don't mind staying in the background and making my main focus praying for you and praying for this church."

"No, Charles. It would be wrong of me to hold you back from your calling as a pastor. Look at all the people who line up after every service to speak with you. You have a true shepherd's heart. Your counseling skills are amazing, especially since you have no formal training in that area. When it comes to pastoring, you're such a natural. Deep in my heart, I know this. About once a month I receive calls from churches asking if we've raised up and trained any spiritual sons who are ready to take on established pastorates. I'd like to direct some of those inquiries your way. I think you're ready."

My drive home was hard. I arrived home rather downcast.

"What's wrong, honey?" Lynn immediately asked. "Does Pastor Dave not think you're ready to take on pastoring the college kids?"

"He actually thinks I'm even more ready than that! He wants to start recommending me to pastoral search committees!"

A few days later, Pastor Dave got a call from a large church in Chicago whose pastor had recently passed away. "This church is one of the largest Charismatic churches in the nation," Pastor Dave said to me. "It's a lot of responsibility, but I think you can handle it."

When I shared with Lynn, it fell flat as a pancake. "I don't wanna leave New York City, and my mom, and my culture. Chicago? I have no burden for Chicago!" She cried a lot for the next few days, and when the opportunity closed, she was so relieved.

Actually, Pastor Dave was the one who closed the door. Wanting to be sure he didn't send one of his spiritual sons onto a Titanic, he called that church's treasurer and asked about its financial health. Turns out, his hunch was right, and the church was over five hundred thousand dollars in the red. "Don't touch that with a ten-foot pole," Pastor Dave told me. But the nest had been stirred, and the tears about leaving had begun.

A few weeks later, I was scheduled to perform a funeral service for a dear member who passed away from HIV. "Look at this," I remarked to my wife as I read the map of where we had to go on Saturday afternoon. "Karla lived near Philadelphia. She drove to Times Square Church three times a week, even when she was really sick." Later in the day, our home phone rang. We were in the middle of dinner so we let the answering machine get it. We could hear the person on the other end say, "Hi, this is Bob. I'm the head of the pastoral search committee at Trinity Assembly in Scottsdale, Arizona. David Wilkerson gave me your number and said I could call you. We've been looking for a pastor for over a year now and..."

Lynn remarked, "Scottsdale, Arizona. I am not moving to Arizona!"

The message continued: "I have a business meeting in Philadelphia this coming Sunday and will be flying in a little early. If you'd like to drive down on Saturday, I'll treat you to dinner and we can talk about this further." He then left his number and hung up.

Lynn and I looked at each other, and she said, "Well, it looks like we'll be in Philadelphia at exactly the same time. How about that?"

"I guess we should look into it," I remarked.

The next Saturday evening we were in a fancy steakhouse talking to Bob about his church. He said, "We've been searching for a pastor for well over a year."

"Why haven't you been able to find one?" I replied with both Tennessee kindness and New York frankness. My boldness choked him up a bit, or perhaps it was just his well-done steak.

"Well," he continued, "we're a unique church. Almost all our members subscribe to Pastor Dave's newsletters, and we really resonate with his messages. We've had Leonard Ravenhill in to do seminars on repentance and revival. There are not that many Bible college graduates who would fit into that type of church. Anyway, I have a guesthouse behind my swimming pool, so why don't you two take an all-expense paid vacation to Scottsdale. If it's not God, I'll still make sure you have an awesome vacation. All I ask of you is that you preach for us on Sunday morning while you're there."

We accepted his invitation, and I polished up the strongest message I've ever preached. Might as well give them the hardest word I had. If they didn't like it, they would eventually not like me, so I figured I had nothing to lose by being totally upfront. The congregation actually loved it. They were tired of the wishy-washy, feel-good, don't-offend-anyone sermons that ministerial candidates usually preach when they "try out" for a pulpit. To my surprise, that afternoon the church met and voted me in as their senior pastor, if I would accept the offer. Lynn felt that the Lord told her, "If you go, I'll bless you." Amazingly, she was ready to pack up and head west.

"I need more time to pray and discuss this with my leaders at Times Square Church," I finally said to Bob and the rest of the eagerly waiting search committee members. "I'll give you an answer in two weeks. Is that OK?"

"Fair enough," they said, and we headed to the Phoenix airport.

The first person I spoke with about Scottsdale was Pastor Bob. I told him about the funeral in Philly, about meeting Bob, how the church had guest speakers like Leonard Ravenhill, and how Lynn felt peace about going.

"So what's the problem, Charles? It seems there's still something major that's bothering you."

"Pastor Bob, you know when I pastored in the South Bronx, the Mott Haven section has the lowest income level in the country. But Scottsdale! Scottsdale is where millionaires and billionaires live."

"I understand. I too was prejudiced against rich people once. I used to avoid wealthy Christians until the Lord showed me how wrong that is and how prejudiced I was against them. I bet if you take that position, you'll find that many of those rich Christian men and women love Jesus just as much as you do."

His words cut to the heart and revealed an area of prejudice in me that I had never seen before. I had taken a lot of pride in not being prejudiced against African Americans, Hispanics, or any other minority. I would often joke about my first church in the Bronx being 50 percent black, 49 percent Hispanic, and 1 percent me. But it would be wrong for me not to go to Scottsdale just because it was a wealthy town. Perhaps I needed to learn how to relate to rich people, just as others need to learn how to appreciate poor minorities. I didn't want to leave Pastor Dave and Pastor Don and Times Square Church, yet I knew I needed to prayerfully consider moving to another strange new world: the Southwest, the suburbs of Phoenix, Arizona.

The next day, I eagerly resumed my regular routines, which included daily Bible reading. I'd been going through the Book of Acts in my New King James Bible, the first time reading through the Bible in that particular version. My mouth opened wide as I read this passage:

> And because the harbor was not suitable to winter in, the majority advised to set sail from there also, if by any means they could reach Phoenix, a harbor of Crete opening toward the southwest and northwest, and winter there (Acts 27:12).

Wow! I didn't ever remember reading about Paul going to Phoenix before! I realized that the King James Version says "Phenice." I grabbed my New King James Version concordance and discovered that was the only listing for Phoenix in the New King James Bible. Not only was it the same spelling as Phoenix, the capital of Arizona, but also I came across that passage right then—not three weeks before or two months later, but right when I was asking the Lord if it was His will for us to move to the Phoenix area. A few more confirmations came in, and Lynn and I were fully convinced that the Lord was opening a new door for us to walk through, an *"opening toward the southwest"* (Acts 27:12).

11

"When you're willing to serve the servants, that's when heavenly promotion comes."

I WAS WALKING WITH PASTOR DAVE AFTER A POWERFUL FRIDAY EVENING service, escorting him back to his nearby apartment in the Worldwide Plaza on 50th Street and Eighth Avenue. Dr. Michael Brown, who was our most regular guest speaker at Times Square Church, had just shared with us his heart's cry for true revival to come to our land. If there ever was an example in our day of a minister of the Gospel receiving the mantle of another, it's Michael Brown walking in Leonard Ravenhill's preaching and writing anointing. I was so deeply stirred by his message that night. As we walked down 51st Street together, I noticed people's reactions to Pastor Dave. They respectfully said, "Hi, Pastor Dave" if they knew who he was. Even if they didn't recognize him, they still nodded their heads in respect as though he were the CEO of a global corporation. There was something in the way he carried himself. He had on a cool-looking leather jacket. As a matter of fact, come to think of it, he always was immaculately dressed—never showy, but never shoddy.

I mentioned to him how much the service blessed me. I don't recall if it was from a song or in the sermon, but something had been said about the life of Joseph from the Book of Genesis. Apparently, Pastor Dave was still contemplating it because he said to me, "Charles, just like with Joseph, when you're willing to serve the servants, that's when heavenly promotion comes. Joseph gladly ministered to Pharaoh's servants in that awful prison, and before he knew it, he was in charge of all of Egypt. God will bless you tremendously if He can trust you." How much of that was directed personally to me and how much was a sermon he was working on I'll never know. The next thing he said, however, was definitely for me.

"Don't get caught up in the numbers game, always striving for a bigger and better ministry. So many young pastors are consumed with packing the people in, but that kind of striving never ends. Bigger is not always better. Be content with what God gives you. I can picture Joseph in that Egyptian prison, finding deep contentment in whatever God allowed him to face and wherever he found himself."

"Pastor Dave, so often when you preach about biblical characters, it's as though you were right there, observing it as an eyewitness. You really bring Bible stories to life!"

"Charles, a sanctified imagination is one of the mightiest weapons in the hands of God. If you want your sermons to be riveting, become addicted to reading, not to watching television. And do what Michael Brown did tonight. Put a lot of Scriptures in your messages. It's almost impossible to put too many Scriptures in a sermon. It's the power of God's Word that breaks hardened hearts. Allow conviction to go deep into people's hearts before you pull the scalpel out. Scripture-filled, convicting sermons are like successful heart surgeries: they save lives."

We stopped at the corner of Eighth Avenue and patiently waited for the traffic light to change. "Pastor Dave, have you ever noticed that a green traffic light is actually many small green light bulbs all clumped closely together in a circle? It's kind of like that when the Lord leads us in a new direction. For instance, I wouldn't have met with the guy from Arizona unless we both were in Philadelphia at exactly the same time. I then found out that Lynn feels peace about moving. That's really amazing given that she's such a New Yorker. And then I ran across in my daily Bible reading that Paul was heading toward Phoenix!"

Pastor Dave suddenly interjected, "Are you sure you want to leave, Charles? No one knows this yet, but Pastor Bob will be leaving soon, and you'll have many more opportunities to preach if you stay. You have the honor of thousands of people here."

"I don't care about the honor of man," I respectfully replied. "I thought you didn't either, Pastor Dave."

"I don't care about it for me, but I care about it for them. You can't lead people into the rich things of God if they don't honor you. It takes years to build a life of honor and just a few minutes of folly to lose it."

"Pastor Dave, there are so many indications that the Lord is opening this new door for me. But if you don't feel good about it... that would definitely be a red flag, a big red flag—like a red light bulb within a green traffic light. I'd have to reconsider the whole thing if you don't feel peace about it."

"I feel peace," Pastor Dave slowly replied. "I'll just...miss you."

"I'll never stop backing you up in prayer, Pastor Dave. No matter where I am, I'll still be a Daniel Nash to you. I love you, Pastor Dave."

"Me too," he replied.

We hugged, and he quickly walked past the concierge's desk. I turned and headed toward my car.

The following day, I arrived at my office on the 38th floor of the skyscraper across the street from Times Square Church. I slowly packed up my last belongings, feeling emotionally numb.

Barbara, Pastor Dave's secretary, called me through the intercom. "Pastor Charles?"

"Yes, Barbara?"

"Pastor Dave would like to see you in his office for a moment."

"OK. Be right there."

As I walked down the long hallway, I saw him standing outside his office with an envelope in his hand. He would usually invite me in, where we would sit down and talk. But not today. It was as though he didn't want to talk too long, lest the goodbyes become too traumatic for either of us. After all, we had said our goodbyes last night. I noticed that he had dark circles under his eyes, as though he hadn't slept a wink the night before. The tiredness on his countenance was such that I opened my mouth to ask if he was OK.

He beat me to it and abruptly said, "I've had quite a talk with the Lord last night. You've worked much harder here than any of us have ever realized, Charles. You've done a lot of things behind the scenes that have been unnoticed by everyone, except for the Lord of course." I hung my head down and took a deep gulp, holding back the welling tears as he continued. "Thanks for all your hard work. Enclosed is a copy of the reference letter I faxed to the pastoral search committee in Arizona and also a gift for you. You'll find that Phoenix is much warmer than here. You and Lynn will need to buy a whole new wardrobe." As I took the envelope, he turned and walked down the hall, past the receptionist, and out the front door of the church offices to the elevators.

I slowly walked back to my office thinking, "Is this really happening?" I closed the door behind me and opened the envelope, not even taking time to sit down. Along with the letter, there was a check for ten thousand dollars. The letter said:

Dear Bob and the Search Committee:

I highly recommend Pastor Charles Simpson. He has a strong holiness message, but it is balanced with great love, mercy and compassion. He is truly a man of prayer, and he knows how to hear from God. We are very reluctant to release him, because he has been such a vital part of our ministry in New York. But about a month ago, the Lord told me it was time to release him, because he would be needed by a congregation.

He would need the oversight of some godly men who would treat him with dignity and advise him in a very compassionate manner. He is teachable and would not be dictatorial. He has yet much to learn, but I believe he is ready to take on a full-time pastorate.

His bondservant,

David Wilkerson

No wonder they so quickly voted me in! I sat down in my chair and put my arms on my desk and my head in my hands. I cried awhile, for various reasons, but mostly because it was final. I was leaving Pastor Dave, my spiritual father. I was leaving Times Square Church, filled with so many dear friends and great memories. The traffic light in front of me turned bright green and the cars behind me were honking. I had to release the brake, press on the gas pedal, and drive on.

12

"Don't ever be a carbon copy of me."

BEFORE I LEFT TIMES SQUARE CHURCH, A LADY NAMED PAT FROM THE congregation gave me a word. Pat and her husband Dick were dear friends, hosting me in their New Jersey home multiple times when I was a single pastor in desperate need of a warm meal and rich fellowship. Pat was a bold lover of truth who always spoke her mind with compassion. When she spoke, I listened. I saw her heading toward me during an anointed worship service at Times Square Church. I was walking down the aisle, as I often left my seat to go up to the balcony or to the back to put out spiritual fires: disorderly drunks, demoniacs, or deranged and noisy people who needed prayer or who needed to be gently and firmly escorted out of the building.

"Charles," she said to me, as she grabbed my arm and whispered into my ear, "you are an Elisha to this Elijah." She looked up at Pastor Dave on the stage. She repeated, "He's Eli-jah, and you're Eli-sha."

Even before they met, God already established that Elisha would be Elijah's successor.[24] Regarding successors, however, Pastor Carter Conlon is doing an awesome job as senior pastor of Times Square Church, Gary Wilkerson is carrying on World Challenge and Please

Pass the Bread, and Don Wilkerson is continuing to help guide the vision and implementation of Teen Challenge. Maybe the mantles of some prophets are so large they must be divided into pieces before being distributed! So what was I to do with a word like that? As a son to a father, I did my best to serve and help Pastor Dave, but I knew I was not called to literally walk in his shoes and his amazing calling. And yet, something in the way Pat gave me that word caused me to take it to the Lord in prayer and diligently study First and Second Kings all over again. Perhaps there was something in that word the Lord wanted me to grasp.

Elijah will always stand out as greater, mightier, and more powerful than almost all the Old Testament prophets, including Elisha. Elijah was unequaled—so much more famous than Elisha, and rightly so. Elijah was the model of what a prophet should be: sold out, dedicated, a true trailblazer. Elisha and many others after him walked on the trail Elijah blazed. I like to ask this Bible trivia question to my students: "Who in the Scriptures raised the dead, multiplied food, and taught that we are to overcome the hatred of our enemies by showing love? And it's someone other than Jesus, someone in the Old Testament." I usually stump all the students to whom I ask this question. That's how overlooked Elisha still is; he's still an unsung hero. He never reached the fame of his mentor. Elisha had to see something in order to receive a double portion of Elijah's spirit, and he saw it—the heavenly chariot taking his master up into glory.[25] And from then on, the reality of the heavenly realm gave him the ability to conquer a particular fear that had plagued Elijah. The difference between these two men can be seen in how each of them handled being surrounded by hostile enemies. The episode with Elijah:

> *Then the king sent to him a captain of fifty with his fifty men. So he went up to him; and there he was, sitting on the top of a hill. And he spoke to him: "Man of God, the*

> *king has said, 'Come down!'" So Elijah answered and
> said to the captain of fifty, "If I am a man of God, then
> let fire come down from heaven and consume you and
> your fifty men." And fire came down from heaven and
> consumed him and his fifty* (2 Kings 1:9-10).

Could it be that Elijah was ministering in that particular moment out of a spirit of fear instead of the Spirit of God? I know it seems disrespectful to even consider such a thing, but if we're not willing to see a prophet's shortcomings, we'll be prone to repeat them. When Jesus's disciples asked Him if they too could call down fire on those who rejected Christ, just like Elijah did to his enemies, Jesus rebuked them, saying, *"You do not know what manner of spirit you are of. For the Son of Man did not come to destroy men's lives but to save them"* (Luke 9:56).

When Elijah was about to toast the third group of fifty, the captain pleaded with him. His lengthy speech stopped Elijah long enough so that he could finally hear the Lord speak to his anxious heart, saying, *"Do not be afraid of him"* (2 Kings 1:15).

> *Again, he sent a third captain of fifty with his fifty men.
> And the third captain of fifty went up, and came and fell
> on his knees before Elijah, and pleaded with him, and
> said to him: "Man of God, please let my life and the life
> of these fifty servants of yours be precious in your sight.
> Look, fire has come down from heaven and burned up
> the first two captains of fifties with their fifties. But let
> my life now be precious in your sight." And the angel of
> the Lord said to Elijah, "Go down with him; do not be
> afraid of him." So he arose and went down with him to
> the king* (2 Kings 1:13-15).

If Elijah had been speaking out of fear, then why did God back him up and send the fire down upon those poor men? It's because when Old Testament prophets spoke, God always backed up their words; otherwise they would have been labeled as false prophets.[26] However, some of Elijah's responses were out of his own fear, rather than from the Spirit of God. And Elisha's double portion, contingent upon seeing the heavenly hosts, enabled him to minister out of love instead of fear toward the hostile enemies who one day surrounded him:

> *Therefore he sent horses and chariots and a great army there, and they came by night and surrounded the city. And when the servant of the man of God arose early and went out, there was an army, surrounding the city with horses and chariots. And his servant said to him, "Alas, my master! What shall we do?" So he answered, "Do not fear, for those who are with us are more than those who are with them." And Elisha prayed, and said, "Lord, I pray, open his eyes that he may see." Then the Lord opened the eyes of the young man, and he saw. And behold, the mountain was full of horses and chariots of fire all around Elisha* (2 Kings 6:14-17).

These same heavenly beings were what Elisha saw at Elijah's parting. Seeing them take Elijah away was the one condition to be met in order for him to receive a double portion. As I have ministered to people on their deathbeds, some of them have seen and spoken to the invisible messengers that have come to escort them home. Witnessing things like that tends to remove the fear of dying from your heart! As the pastor in charge of the hospital visitation ministry and the AIDS ministry of a large urban church, I have seen many more deathbed experiences than I ever expected. The one that blessed me the most, however, was when I flew home to Tennessee to be with my dying mom.

My younger sister, Bertie, called and said the doctors were not expecting Mom to live through the night. She had a heart attack, it seemed, and was barely hanging on. All of her twelve kids were in the process of driving to her. When I arrived at the hospital, Linda told me that Mom's lungs were filling up with liquid, her kidneys had failed, and it wouldn't be long now. She was in ICU, of course, so they were only allowing one family member to stay with her, alternating every half hour.

"Charles, you want to see her next?"

"Yes."

"Get ready," my sister Linda said. "It's five minutes till 4:00. And also, prepare yourself. Mom says she's seeing angels in the room with her, but it's probably just the medication."

One of my agnostic brothers objected, saying, "Maybe it really is angels!"

When I walked into the room and went over to Mom, I was not even sure if she recognized me. And I heard that dreaded death rattle I'd witnessed so many times in hospitals in New York City. Suddenly, Mom straightened up and stared at something behind and above me. She said, "Why, yes, I do agree that would be the best thing. Yes, I am. That would be fine." There's no doubt that Mom was speaking with a being from another world. Mom is a believer, and there was no alarm. It was as though that conversation was prepping her for Heaven. "I don't know," Mom continued to speak to this being who was invisible to my eyes.

My faith was shooting through the roof. My hospital visitation experience kicked into gear, along with the determination to pray in faith for healing for all who would allow me to do so.

"Mom," I exclaimed. "Mom!"

"Yes, Charles. What is it, son?"

"Mom, do you want to be healed, or do you want to go home to Heaven?"

"I want to be healed."

"OK. Let's pray." I then commanded, in the authority of Jesus's name, that her kidneys start working, her lungs clear up, and her heart be healed. Nothing seemed to happen so I finished spending time with her, kissed her goodbye, and left because it was another sibling's turn. Later that evening, they decided to move Mom to her own room so all the family could gather around her. When one of my sisters asked the nurse why they were not taking the IV up to her room, she gently said she wouldn't make it through the night so it was totally unnecessary. The next morning, Mom woke up hungry for breakfast! It took a few days, but her kidneys started functioning again and her lungs cleared up. When they tested her heart, they found out that she didn't have a heart attack after all. Actually, a heart valve had ruptured. After repairing it, she was soon ready to go to rehab, and then back home in a few months.

When I saw my mom (who is not an exaggerator) speaking with an angel, my faith in God soared and I prayed the prayer of faith over her almost effortlessly.[27] Elisha knew beyond a shadow of a doubt that the chariots and the angels of God would protect him. He had seen them with his very own eyes! He then won his enemies over with love, providing a vast banquet for them. The conclusion of that episode is those people who attacked Elisha did not attack him or Israel again.[28]

But how does all that apply here? Pastor Dave was the most fearless Christian I've ever met. Another word perhaps describes some of his responses, as mentioned in a previous chapter: frustration. Personally, I feel that we (the Body of Christ) dumped so much junk on him that his soul was vexed beyond what it should have been. Am I saying that some of his messages were tainted? God forbid. He was the most untainted person I've ever met—untainted as in James's description that pure religion includes caring for the orphans and widows and keeping oneself unspotted from the world.[29] I'm saying he told me not to emulate him to the point that I would copy his frailties and weaknesses. As he told Nicky Cruz one time, "Don't ever be a carbon copy of me. Instead, be a carbon copy of Jesus." Even seeing Pastor Dave's weaknesses up close and firsthand for years, he still was the strongest believer I've ever known, by far.

In a desire to see that I, one of his spiritual sons, would grow to my fullest potential, he warned me about becoming a carbon copy of himself and thus inheriting his tendency to become too frustrated with the Body of Christ. Because of much frustration over their shortcomings, Pastor Dave and his staff (including me) labeled many nationally known ministers as charlatans and even false prophets. But the truth is, most of them were just flawed men and women like us. When people around the world flooded Pastor Dave's mailbox with videos and CDs of the ministers in question, I assure you, those videos and CDs did not reflect the speakers at their best, but at their worst. Take any minister at his worst, quote him out of context, magnify his shortcomings and blind spots, and you can make a monster (or even a heretic) out of just about anyone.

Pastor Dave was a holy man, a true saint (in the biblical sense of the word) and yet, he'd be the first to point out he was far from perfect.[30] And neither was his mentor, Leonard Ravenhill. Mack Tomlinson recently completed a wonderful book on the life of Brother Ravenhill called *In Light of Eternity*. As I came to the section about earthen vessels, I could not help but think of the similarities between these two spiritual giants. The rest of this chapter is an excerpt from his book.[31]

Passionate Preachers as Earthen Vessels

Leonard shows us that true preaching comes through imperfect men...He had imperfections and he knew it. He knew all believers were still growing in grace, including him. Sometimes his courage and zeal caused him to speak in a way that was wrong and unnecessarily harsh. Like all preachers, he was an earthen vessel because he was a human being. He was a clay pot into which God poured great things. Apart from the man Christ Jesus, no perfect man has ever lived. Even though Ravenhill was a holy and righteous man, I never fell into the trap of wrongly idolizing him or viewing him unrealistically. He had imperfections, flaws, imbalances, and weaknesses. This is not to lessen who he was. It is only to view him properly, an earthen vessel in whom was a divine treasure.

It is good to have spiritual heroes we emulate. But idolizing men is a different thing altogether. It is a subtle trap to be avoided. Scripture says, *"Stop regarding man, in whose nostrils is breath, for of what account is he?"* (Isaiah 2:22). We are to appreciate, honor and respect God's men, but never idolize or view them as perfect. Leonard himself shared this view. He loved God's preachers and God's servants, but he learned to view them all correctly. Ravenhill was conscious of the fact that he was perceived as being too strict, narrow, and even judgmental. Speaking of Martin Luther, Leonard said,

> I have empathy with Luther when he said, "I was born to fight devils and factions; it is my business to remove obstructions, to cut down thorns, to fill up quagmires, and to open and make straight paths. If I must have some failing, let me rather speak the truth with too great severity than once to act the hypocrite and conceal the truth."

This reveals why he spoke as he did. Leonard was so protective of souls hearing the truth that he wanted nothing to interfere with the Holy Spirit working in their hearts. His motives were right, even if his methods were questionable at times. Even his unwise zeal put the fear of God in people. The lesson here is clear. Every Christian must remember that the best preachers are still men and must not be exalted.

13

"I can't preach tonight until I do something first."

HAVE I LIVED MY CHRISTIAN LIFE (SO FAR) AS ONE OF PASTOR DAVID'S spiritual sons? Some of the Jews in Jesus's day exclaimed, "Abraham is our father," and Jesus came back with, "If he were your father, you would walk in his steps" (see John 8:39). Paul taught that we all are sons of Abraham, at least those of us who walk by faith, as he walked.[32] Pastor Dave's faith was quite amazing. Many times in our pastoral staff prayer meetings, I heard expressions from a deep well of genuine faith within his heart. "Lord," he'd pray quite loudly, "we need our own theater," or "Lord, we need fifty thousand dollars for building repairs," or "Lord, show us where the root of this problem stems from," and everyone in the room knew the answer was already on its way.

We have a tendency to worship our heroes, partly because doing so gets us off the hook. If God especially and uniquely endowed them, we could never reach their level of faith, so why even try? Pastor Dave would object to that type of faulty thinking, and he would object even more strongly to our tendency to worship him as though his giftings were not available to all who would walk in his steps.

It's true that there surely was a deep impartation of faith given to him, probably handed down from his godly grandparents and parents. If you recall from *The Cross and the Switchblade,* when David was twelve years old he prayed the prayer of faith that immediately healed his very sick father.

Paul said to Timothy, *"...I call to remembrance the genuine faith that is in you, which dwelt first in your grandmother Lois and your mother Eunice, and I am persuaded is in you also. Therefore I remind you to stir up the gift of God which is in you through the laying on of my hands"* (2 Tim. 1:5-6). Although Timothy received an impartation from his godly line, he still had the responsibility to stir up the gift of God. A heritage of faith was handed down to this spiritual giant, for sure. But that's not the only or even the main reason for David Wilkerson's strong faith as seen through his fervent prayers, his powerful sermons, and especially his many accomplishments for the Kingdom of God: birthing Teen Challenge, World Challenge, and Times Square Church. (All three of these ministries have touched and are still touching countless lives for Christ.) After being told in many ways and at various times that I am called to "walk in the footsteps of David Wilkerson," I believe what the Lord primarily wants from me is to simply obey the admonition from Hebrews chapter 13:

> *Remember your leaders who taught you the word of God. Think of all the good that has come from their lives, and follow the example of their faith* (Hebrews 13:7 NLT).

After endeavoring to follow in his footsteps for over three decades now, I'd like to share the ways I saw David Wilkerson stir up the gift of faith.

One: Pastor Dave was always listening to God.

It's common knowledge that he would consistently spend from midnight until 2:00 A.M. every day with the Lord, praying and prayerfully reading God's Word. We read about this in *The Cross and the Switchblade.* I had forgotten about that, and when I joined Times Square Church's weekly pastoral prayer meetings that began every Tuesday morning at 10:00 A.M., I was surprised to see that Pastor Dave looked like he had just rolled out of bed! The next few weeks it seemed even more like this was the case, and I just couldn't understand how a man who insisted all staff members have a prayer life could come to the office without spending time with the Lord first. I guess I wear my feelings on my sleeve because the fourth Tuesday Pastor Dave said to me, "Do I look like I just rolled out of bed? Well, I did. I'm not a morning person. That's why I pray from midnight till 2:00 A.M. every day."

As Pastor Dave faithfully spent that time in prayer, his opened Bible was always there. He would talk to God, and God would talk back through His Word. Simple, basic stuff, but how many of us remain in that place spiritually where God can speak to us daily? As Pastor Dave constantly reminded us through his sermons (such as "A Conspiracy of Interruptions"), if we waste hours watching television, our much-needed time with Christ will be compromised.[33]

Two: Pastor Dave was pliable in God's hands.

He changed a lot in the six years I worked closely with him. He probably grew more than anyone else I knew at Times Square Church. That's a remarkable statement! Some spiritual leaders see no need to grow because they are so near perfection in their own eyes. Whenever God dealt with Pastor Dave about something that he needed to change or repent of or start doing, he would humbly submit and allow the Spirit of God to change him. Only a handful of famous musicians remain famous for long because they often stop developing and growing as musicians. Perhaps they get too caught up in their successes. But a handful of musicians seem to reinvent themselves every few years and thus continue to reach closer to their fullest potential as artists. That takes pliability, a trait that is rare among both musicians and Christian leaders. We either get too caught up in our successes or too down about not being successful enough. Not Pastor Dave.

Not long after starting Times Square Church, he read verses in the Bible about not neglecting to feed the hungry ones among us.[34] He immediately started a feeding program through a mobile van, aptly called The Raven Truck, which is still going strong today.

Three: He was a faithful steward of his giftings.

From my limited perspective, these are the giftings that I feel Pastor Dave had: the gift of an evangelist, the gift of faith and miracles, the gift of a prophet, and the gift of pastor with a shepherd's heart for God's people. He also had apostolic giftings for sure, as seen in the many ministries God used him to birth. When he arrived in New York City the first time, the only gift that was in full operation was the gift of faith and miracles. He was given a measure of faith that he nurtured and exercised through decades of seeing the hand of God meet his needs and those for whom he prayed. He didn't start out by praying for the sixteen million dollars needed to buy the Mark Hellinger Theatre. He started by believing God for the gas money to get from Pennsylvania to New York City and back!

Four: Pastor Dave was persistent.

Day in and day out, week in and week out, year in and year out, he would be about the Father's business. When God would give him a mission, hell could not stop him. He might have to tweak things, try new things, and experiment a bit before the victory would come, but he would not quit. He would serve God on the mountaintop peaks of spiritual breakthroughs, as well as in the valleys and the plains of day-to-day spiritual consistency. Sometimes when we share our mountaintop experiences in the Lord, we neglect to mention the days, months, and even years of mundane persistence that may occur between them.

Five: Pastor Dave was truly a godly man.

If those who knew Pastor Dave personally were asked to describe him in one adjective, most of us would use the word *godly*. Perfect? No. Godly? Absolutely! Before coming on staff at Times Square Church, many of the leaders with whom I worked had hidden ungodly behaviors that eventually surfaced, causing enormous pain to everyone around them. I was actually reluctant to become a behind-the-scenes associate pastor, apprehensive of becoming disillusioned and disappointed once again. But I wasn't. Pastor Dave was just as godly on his days off and during seasons of intense pressure as he was when he stood in the pulpit as God's mouthpiece. Pure faith doesn't flow through impure vessels.

Six: Pastor Dave was willing to admit his mistakes publicly.

When Pastor Dave hosted a leadership conference in Manhattan in 2002, this surely was a time to boast in the Lord to all his peers as to how faithful God had been to him. The packed meetings were held at the fancy Radio City Music Hall in Manhattan. People from all over the world (and some former staff members including myself) came to be spiritually fed and stirred, once again, by his words and his godly example. So what did this great man of God do? When it was his time to speak, he talked about his failures as the leader of his church staff and about how harsh he had been in the past to some of those staff members, and he publicly asked for our forgiveness! Pastor Dave was as tough as nails, but what general isn't? Isn't that par for the course for all true generals? And yet there were times, for whatever reasons, when Pastor Dave was too harsh. Whether it was out of frustration or intolerance, most of us who worked closely with

Pastor Dave knew that when he got angry, he could become profoundly severe. There were times he missed it in his prophetic words (or perhaps it's just a matter of the timing being off). Unlike most of the leaders who silently hide away when they miss it prophetically, Pastor Dave would openly, humbly, and publicly apologize.

Seven: Pastor Dave could laugh at himself.

Some people take themselves way too seriously, but Pastor Dave had a sense of humor that was often pointed toward himself. He was a serious man. His seriousness wasn't so much inward as it was outward. He lived, spoke, and preached as though there's a Heaven to gain and a hell to shun for all he preached to, spoke with, and encountered. Pastor Dave always listened to God, was pliable in His hands, was faithful to his duties, vulnerable, humble, and he had a healthy sense of humor regarding his frailties. He was always real.

Eight: Pastor Dave deliberately took himself off our pedestals.

This eighth characteristic of a man of God who enjoys ever-increasing faith (knocking himself off the pedestals on which we put him) can best be shared by describing a scene that I'll never forget. It wasn't the first or last time I saw him deliberately do this, but it was the most memorable:

The Mark Hellinger Theatre is literally packed. It's a few minutes before 6:00 P.M., and about a hundred of us are at the altar, fervently asking God to bless this Sunday evening service and everyone here tonight. The large maroon theater curtain slowly, but very noticeably, begins to open as someone backstage pulls it up by a rope. I look up and see Pastor Gwen Warren (the choir director) and the choir singing a soul-stirring song about the Mighty One of Israel. Those of us at the altar quickly find our seats, and I walk up the side steps and find my place on the stage, along with the other pastors.

I used to sit directly behind Pastor Dave, but he asked me to sit on the front row since I'm an associate pastor. I would rather sit behind him though. His chair is closest to the edge of the stage, and sometimes I envision a madman attacking him with a knife or a gun. I've already decided how I will respond if it ever happens, God forbid. That bullet or blade will have to go through me first, and then I'm sure one of the other staff members will be able to wrestle him to the ground before he gets another chance at Pastor Dave. I'm standing next to Pastor Harry, and to his left are Pastors Bob, Don, and Dave. I look up in the balcony and see my dear wife sitting in her regular place. The anointed music fills our ears as we sing with all our hearts to our risen Lord. I look out across the theater and see hungry people: people hungry for Jesus, hungry for His Word, hungry for His presence. The awesome presence of God begins to fill the place and our hearts. During the fourth song, Pastor Dave walks over to me and hands me a large stack of prayer request cards that were filled out by parishioners before the service. He says to me, "You can go and pray after this song."

The song ends, and we are at the most holy moment in the service. The Lord's presence is so thick it seems like you can slice it. "Oh Lord," I pray silently even before I reach the pulpit microphone, "please don't let me ruin this holy moment. Lord, what would You have me pray about, and how should I pray?" And every time, the Lord would answer that cry for help. I didn't realize that like Samuel in the temple, I was learning how to hear God's voice on a regular basis through this. As I reach the mic, I say, "Let's pray," and then I pray from the depths of my soul for the needs on the cards and whatever else the Lord puts on my heart.

We sing another song, and then one of the other pastors makes announcements regarding upcoming events. After one last song, Pastor Dave will begin his sermon. During this last song, when all of us are standing and singing, Pastor Dave begins to walk to the pulpit. He looks over at us with a glance that says, "Listen carefully to what

I'm about to say." He grabs the microphone and says, "I can't preach tonight until I do something first. Honey, where are you?" he says as he scans the crowded balcony for his wife. Gwen raises and then waves her arms to help expedite his search. "Honey, I am so sorry. Please forgive me for yelling at you."

He looks down at all the shocked onlookers and says, "When I left the apartment and got into the elevator, the Lord spoke to me. He said, 'David, why is it that whenever Gwen gets angry it's demonic, but whenever *you* get angry it's always righteous indignation?'" He then lets out hearty laughter at himself! His brother Don is the first one to join him in his laughing spell. Pastor Dave looks over at him and says, "There's my older brother laughing with me, or is it *at* me? I can't tell which one it is!" (Pastor Don is eight years younger than his brother.) By now, the entire place is laughing. None of us, to be sure, are laughing at Pastor Dave. We are all laughing with him as he yanks himself off the pedestal of perfection on which many of us put him.

Pastor Dave then preaches an evangelistic message, which causes the unsaved to come to the altar under deep conviction. They hear the Heavenly Father telling them to forsake their pigpen of sin and come home to a new life in Christ. The sermon also contains pastoral comfort regarding how deeply the Lord cherishes us and how we can trust His unchanging love, no matter how bad things look. I forget what text he used for the sermon that evening, but I'll never forget he pre-sermon illustration of humbling himself before his wife and his congregation.

To walk in his footsteps of faith, we must always be listening to God, remain pliable in the Lord's hands, be a faithful steward of our giftings, be persistent, live a genuinely godly life, be willing to openly admit our mistakes, learn how to laugh at ourselves, and take ourselves off any man-made pedestals. And yet, this list doesn't adequately tell the whole story. Pastor Dave didn't just live a godly life. He also lived a supernatural one. I personally know hundreds of men and women of God who consistently walk in these eight godly steps who have never killed one single spiritual giant, much less a whole list of them like Pastor Dave did. If we desire to walk in his footsteps, it's going to take the supernatural touch of God upon our lives, similar to what he experienced.

14

"Get what Daniel got— the touch of God!"

DAVID WILKERSON WAS SO MUCH MORE THAN JUST A GODLY EXAMPLE to be encouraged by. He was also a forerunner, way ahead of his time. Like Jeremiah the prophet, he saw calamity coming during times of ease, *and* he saw blessings coming during times of calamity! He preached in the 1980s about a dangerous "Christless Pentecost" coming to the Church, one in which the manifestations of the Holy Spirit would eclipse the person of Christ. And then, during his later days, he saw glimpses of what I would call a Christ-filled Pentecost, where believers would be so genuinely consumed by the Holy Spirit that He would share God's very heart and soul with them. On the Day of Pentecost, to explain what was happening, Peter quoted Joel's famous prophecy:

> *It shall come to pass in the last days, says God, that I will pour out My Spirit on all flesh; your sons and your daughters shall prophesy, your young men shall see visions, your old men shall dream dreams* (Acts 2:17).

I believe there's more here than we've ever seen, ever appropriated, or ever personally experienced. The Holy Spirit gives us more than the ability to prophesy. If interpreted by Numbers 12:6, the experience of dreams and visions given to the young and old refers to God giving New Testament believers a prophet's revelation of the personhood and heart of God Himself.

> *...If there is a prophet among you, I the Lord make Myself known to him in a vision; I speak with him in a dream"* (Numbers 12:6 ESV).

What made a prophet's ministry in the Scriptures so amazing was not that they could accurately prophesy, but that they would shed the very tears of God, experiencing the pain and heartache the Lord felt over His wayward people. Yes, a Christ-filled Pentecost is coming, when Moses's heart-cry will be fulfilled: *"...I wish that all the Lord's people were prophets and that the Lord would put His Spirit on them!"* (Num. 11:29 NIV) Pastor Dave's sermon titled "The Touch of God" was a message he preached often and one he felt very passionate about for various reasons:

- He knew it was the supernatural touch of God upon him that enabled him to slay giants, conquering what others considered unconquerable.

- He knew that the same God who used his life desires to use you and me beyond our imagination, beyond our dreams, and way beyond our own natural abilities.

- He had a hope that in these last days, God would raise up an army of believers who would experience the touch of God upon their lives, setting them on fire for the Lord, enabling them to reach a mighty harvest of souls.

The touch of God first came upon David Wilkerson when he was eight years old and he received Christ as his Savior. The second time was when he received the call to New York City:

> The Holy Spirit came on me and said, "David, I'm calling you to prayer." I said, "Yes, God"—and I began to weep like I never wept. After three days, I felt the burden of the Lord in a way I'd never felt before. Then one day, I went home, picked up *LIFE Magazine,* and saw the faces of seven young men who'd committed murder. And God said, "Go to New York. This is what it's all about."[35]

Years later, the touch of God came upon him again when the Lord called him to return to New York City to raise up a church in one of the most famous and busiest crossroads in the world, Times Square.

> While walking down 42nd Street at midnight, Pastor David Wilkerson's heart broke over what he saw. At that time, Times Square was populated mainly by prostitutes and pimps, runaways, drug addicts and hustlers, along with live peep shows and X-rated movie houses. Pastor David cried out for God to do something—anything—to help the physically destitute and spiritually dead people he saw. Recalling that life-changing night, Pastor David says, "I saw 9-, 10- and 11-year-old kids bombed on crack cocaine. I walked down 42nd Street and they were selling crack. Len Bias, the famous basketball player, had just died of a crack overdose, and the pusher was yelling, 'Hey, I've got the stuff that killed Len.' I wept and prayed, 'God, You've got to raise up a testimony in this hellish place....' The answer was not what I wanted to hear: 'Well, you know the city. You've been here. You

do it.'" Pastor David obeyed God. He opened Times Square Church in 1987.[36]

In "The Touch of God," Pastor Dave uses the example of Daniel, a man of prayer who became, at the urgings of the Lord, a man of intense prayer:

> The reason many Christians today are confused is because they have not pursued the Lord in prayer. They have not given time or sought His face. I tell you, if you will set your heart like Daniel and get the burden for God's glory—not giving up, and going on until you can go no further—you will get what Daniel got: the touch of God! ...If you want only to be saved—only to have daily devotions and to do what is right—then this message is not for you. But if you hunger for more of God, if you want Him to lay hold of your life, there is a price! Consider the price Daniel paid: Daniel *"set his face to seek the Lord with all his strength and will"* (9:3).[37]

The supernatural touch of God is initiated with the Lord calling us to a place of extraordinary prayer. Jonathan Edwards, the revivalist who spearheaded the First Great Awakening in America in the 1700s, taught that when God has something extraordinary to accomplish through His Church, He first calls His people to extraordinary prayer. In Zechariah 12:10, when God is about to accomplish great things, He begins by a remarkable outpouring of *"the Spirit of grace and supplication"* upon His people, producing deep and desperate prayer. If I were to summarize David Wilkerson's walk with God in one biblical verse, it would be from the words of another David: *"When You said, 'Seek My face,' my heart said to You, 'Your face, Lord, I will seek'"* (Ps. 27:8). David Wilkerson's life is an example of someone seeking the face of God until the Holy Spirit came and distinctly touched his heart and spoke to his soul, giving him a divine burden and divine instructions over and over throughout his life.

To say there's a price to pay for the touch of God can be misleading if we misinterpret it as saying we earn something. We certainly don't earn God's blessings. And yet, millions of believers are living non-supernatural lives because we never stir ourselves up to "take hold of God" (see Isa. 64:7). Or perhaps we've never been told there is a supernatural walk awaiting all those who desire to be mightily used of the Lord. David Wilkerson's example declares that a scrawny country preacher with the touch of God can effectively minister in New York City to gang members and drug addicts, as well as to Wall Street executives. As his brother Don said, "David's life can be summarized by saying, 'God can use anyone to save anyone,'" meaning even a country preacher can be used by God to reach hardened gang leaders like Nicky Cruz.

It's one thing to be used in the charismatic gifts of the Spirit such as prophecy, and it's quite another to become someone with the heart of a prophet. Pastor Dave, while pastoring a small church in Pennsylvania, began to move in the supernatural giftings of prophesying and words of knowledge, and the crowds came to marvel. But that was just the beginning. Gary Wilkerson wrote in his father's biography that Pastor Dave would walk into Teen Challenge in Brooklyn and give accurate prophetic words to some very surprised students! I personally received many prophetic words from him over the years, things that only God could know.

But then God began to share His heart with him, and he got a prophet's perspective on the Personhood of God. He understood and felt God's broken heart over our sins against Him, and especially our idolatry. For instance, God wept through Jeremiah the prophet as He suffered the pain caused by the spiritual adultery of Israel. Commenting on Jeremiah 2:32, David Wilkerson wrote:

*The Lord asks: Can a maid forget her ornaments or a bride her attire? Yet My people have forgotten Me days without number...*The Lord has put His pain in Scripture for all the world to see! Every generation has read about it. Yet, why would the Lord tell the whole world about such neglect? Shouldn't lovers' differences be kept quiet? No—He wants us to know how hurt He is! He tells the whole world because He is so heartbroken by our behavior! Jeremiah was weeping with holy tears that weren't his own. Indeed, this prophet actually heard God speak of His own weeping, broken heart.[38]

Right before starting Times Square Church, David Wilkerson and Bob Phillips (who would soon join him as an amazing Bible teacher) met together in Texas. Here's what Gary wrote about that insightful meeting:

[Bob says,] "We spent three days together...going through the Scriptures. There's a passage in Ezekiel 44 that's a pretty hard one. It talks about God's people breaking covenant with Him. I'd been preaching from that chapter in a lot of my messages, and David wanted me to share my insights with him." In the passage, God allows his priests to preach the wrong message, so the people would be fed the unholy things they clamored for.

As Bob spoke about the passage, my dad grew quiet. They were sitting at a small table in Dad's hotel room. Suddenly, my father slid out of his chair and onto the floor. "He just fell over," Bob says. "He curled up in a fetal position and began to weep and weep and weep. He was feeling the consequences of that passage of Scripture, and he was crying for the nation."

Bob was dumbstruck. "As I looked at David, I was still upright. All I could think was, I've been preaching this message for a while, but it has never affected me the way it's affecting this man right now. I remember having this thought: 'He's feeling what God feels—and I want that.' I saw a man who not only carried the burden of God, but was deeply impacted by it. That was David's tenderness. He was thinking and feeling with God's heart."[39]

No wonder the Times Square Church pulpit became a platform from which a genuine prophet ministered to the entire nation!

David Wilkerson knew that the touch of God is available to every hungry believer, and he longed for the day when an outpouring of God's Spirit would cause a whole generation of giant-killing believers to be raised up. Who will reach the unsaved Nicky Cruzes of our generation? Who will rise up and slay the cultural and spiritual giants that society has deemed unconquerable? Who is hungry for an outpouring that turns us into people carrying a prophet's revelation of the majesty, heart, and pain of God?

Are we truly willing to follow in David Wilkerson's footsteps, or are we content to be barren believers? In the Old Testament, it was a disgrace for women, such as Hannah, to be barren, to be unable to bear children (see 1 Sam. 1:11). And under the New Covenant, it's a disgrace (in my opinion) for Spirit-filled believers to be barren, to spend our entire lives without receiving and developing a heavenly burden from the Lord. Paul likened carrying these divine burdens to being a woman in labor:

My little children, for whom I labor [travail] in birth again until Christ is formed in you (Galatians 4:19).

It appears that Paul first travailed in prayer for their salvation, and then again for their maturity in Christ. Travailing in prayer is a holy thing, a supernatural work of God as He imparts to His praying men and women a particular burden with a built-in anointing to pray it through to victory. The burdens of the world (and our flesh and the enemy) weigh us down, but burdens birthed from Heaven energize us and empower us to pray until we know the victory has been won. Teen Challenge was birthed in that type of prayer, and so was Times Square Church. All true ministry is birthed in prayer. Don Wilkerson, in a recent sermon entitled "Going into Labor," said:

> When I grew up, there were days during the week we were not allowed to play inside, because those were the days my father, a pastor, prepared for his messages. One day, I forgot and ran into the house with my friend to get a ball glove. Inside the house, my friend suddenly stopped and had a look of fright on his face. He nervously asked, "What's that noise?" There were groaning sounds coming from upstairs. It was my father praying. I said to my buddy, "Oh, it's just my dad praying." That sound was as familiar and common to me as any other sound in the house. When my brother David spent time in prayer rather than watch TV, something was being birthed in the spirit realm. He didn't know what it was, but in due time it was revealed. He happened to pick up a magazine and read the story of a street gang in Manhattan who killed a crippled boy named Michael Farmer. The Holy Spirit put a burden on him that he could not let go. And as they say—the rest is history.[40]

What does God want to birth into the world through the womb of our prayer lives? Let's learn to sit at the feet of the Lord and offer Him our hearts and lives, just like David Wilkerson did over and over. And then we will be amazed by what God does through us. Then we can be sure that we have followed in the footsteps of David Wilkerson. More importantly, we can be confident that we are pleasing the Lord. For the entire length of my Christian walk (over thirty-nine years), David Wilkerson's example has always been set before me. On many occasions, I made the immature mistake of trying to follow in his exact steps, which I am not called or equipped to do. For instance, in my first church plant in the Bronx, I tried to copy Times Square Church instead of developing our own identity as a daughter church.

When I began working at Brooklyn Teen Challenge, Pastor Don taught me to "look for patterns" when dealing with students. In other words, we all make mistakes, but it's continuous, negative patterns that need to be addressed. On the positive side, it's the godly patterns of David Wilkerson's walk with God from which we all can learn. I saw a positive and continuous cycle in Pastor Dave. He diligently sought God until the Lord stirred him deeply and brought him into "birthing prayer." As in the natural, so in the spiritual: intimacy produces conception. Once a burden from Heaven was prayed through and a ministry was birthed, Pastor Dave would then ride the wave of the Holy Spirit as that ministry developed and produced much fruit. Listen to Pastor Dave's passionate prayer for that type of outpouring:

> When the Lord touches someone, that person is driven to his knees. He then becomes intimate with Christ. And out of that intimacy, he receives fresh revelation from Heaven. [But] we do not want the discipline of being shut in with God. We don't want to lose sleep, we don't want to fast. We want to settle for the status quo. God, wake us up! Let some of us get so hungry to be touched by Your hand, so set on fire and burdened for Your will and purpose, that You will come forth and pour out Your Spirit mightily![41]

From his sermon "A Call to Anguish":

> If you set your heart to pray, God's going to come and start sharing His heart with you. When God determined

to recover a ruined situation (as in the days of Nehemiah), He would seek out a praying man, and He'd take him down into the waters of anguish and literally baptize him in anguish.... If He gives you His burden, He's going to give you His peace to accompany it. He'll never let your heart be broken without all the oil you need for total healing.[42]

Let's follow in David Wilkerson's footsteps by claiming for ourselves the scriptural promise the Lord gave him when Teen Challenge was first birthed:

> *Those who sow in tears shall reap in joy. He who continually goes forth weeping, bearing seed for sowing, shall doubtless come again with rejoicing, bringing his sheaves with him* (Psalms 126:5-6).

David Wilkerson's incredible gift of faith wasn't focused mainly on his own needs. The DNA of his faith (and of Teen Challenge) was "faith for souls," that is, the belief that God can and will save people, no matter how hard their hearts had become or how deep their bondages were. *"With God all things are possible,"* Jesus said (Matt. 19:26; Mark 10:27). And He also said, *"If you have faith...nothing will be impossible for you"* (Matt. 17:20).

15

"Something takes your life, and suddenly you're in glory!"

ON APRIL 27, 2011, I HEARD THE NEWS THAT PASTOR DAVE WAS SUD-denly gone, having died in a car wreck somewhere in rural Texas. Times Square Church soon posted information on their website regarding a memorial service they were planning. Since people from all over the world were expected to come, they offered courtesy seating for those who knew Pastor Dave personally. I was instructed to arrive an hour early and find one of the ushers in a light blue jacket, who would then inform my wife and me about which entrance to use to enter the building for the service. I found an usher and told him that I had courtesy seating, and he told us to go to the entrance on the side of the building, the same door I once used to go to my dressing room apartment when I lived in the back of the church many years ago.

As we stood in line, I noticed Pastor Dave's secretary, Barbara, was at the door with a clipboard in hand, always the quintessential secretary. Suddenly, I turned around to see who had joined the line behind us, and there was Pastor Don with his wife Cindy and their kids: Julie, Todd, and Kristy, and their spouses.

"Pastor Don," I exclaimed, "it's so good to see you after so many years!"

"And who are you?" he replied.

"Charles! Charles Simpson."

"Charles! How are you and Lynn?"

"We're doing fine." Lynn and I said hi to Cindy and their kids, and then it was our time to enter the building. I turned and greeted Barbara.

"Hi there, Charles. It's great to see you and Lynn, but this line is for family members only."

"I'm so sorry, Barbara. The usher told us to come here."

"No problem. The courtesy seating line is over there at the front entrance, on the left."

As we got on the correct line, my wife said, "That was embarrassing. I'm glad you explained to Barbara that we were just following the usher's directions."

"He didn't even recognize me," I quietly lamented.

"Charles," my dear wife replied, "did you see the grief on Pastor Don's face? Don't take it personally, honey. He probably won't recognize a lot of familiar faces today."

We sat with our dear friend Michael Brown, who, like many sitting in Times Square Church's beautiful sanctuary, flew in for the occasion. It was the most inspirational memorial service I've ever witnessed. The heartfelt memories shared by Pastor Dave's family and the current Times Square Church pastors had us laughing one minute and weeping the next. Especially moving was the video clip of a sermon in which Pastor Dave exclaimed:

> You see, there's something down deep in my heart that says, "Come what may...the devil can't kill me, can't kill you, without God's permission. And if God permits it,

instant glory!" Something takes your life, and suddenly you're in glory! Hallelujah! Thank You, Jesus!

Afterward, many people lingered around to talk and catch up with old friends. I simply sat there, still feeling the hot tears that made a path from my eyes down to the bottom of my chin. Lynn remarked, "There's Pastor Don over there in the front, talking with people."

"He didn't even recognize me," I repeated as though I never heard Lynn's earlier comments. She affectionately put her hand on top of mine, and that small gesture seemed to snap me out of my little pity party. I looked over at her and smiled, and then I suddenly said, "Wait here, honey. I'm going to try this again." I attempted to make a beeline to Pastor Don, but many old friends and acquaintances kept greeting me on the way. I finally made it to the front, but he was gone. I turned around to head back to my seat, and Pastor Don turned around from somewhere and we almost ran right into each other.

"Charles," he said enthusiastically, "so sorry I didn't recognize you. I knew the line was family only, and that's what threw me off. You don't look like any of my relatives. Not even a distant cousin!" I made a few remarks about how inspiring the memorial service was, just as Pastor Dave's life was. Pastor Don informed me that he moved back to the city and was serving once again as the director of the original Brooklyn Teen Challenge. He handed me his business card, and I gave him mine. He then said his family was waiting for him, and he left.

When I arrived home that evening, I got on my computer and began to write this manuscript. And for the next week I spent every free moment remembering and writing about the many ways and times that Pastor David Wilkerson blessed my life.

The very day and hour I finished the first draft of this manuscript (with the exception of the final chapters), I got an e-mail from

Pastor Don in which he simply wrote, "Charles, what are you doing right now?"

"Right at this moment?" I wrote back, startled at the timing of his question. "Well," I replied, "I'm actually finishing my fifth book called *Walking in the Footsteps of David Wilkerson.*"

"Call me," he simply replied back.

I called the number on his business card, and he asked if I'd like to have lunch with him in Brooklyn that coming Friday. And before I knew it, I was sitting with Pastor Don in an Italian restaurant named Graziella's in the Fort Greene section of Brooklyn, a few blocks from Teen Challenge. After we ordered lunch and the waitress left, he said, "So Charles, I know we've talked a few times since you left Times Square Church. But fill me in. What have you been doing since then?"

"My goodness," I began, "it's been eighteen years since I left Times Square Church! Let's see, by God's grace I've planted five churches: in Arizona, the Bronx, Queens, Manhattan, and then again in Queens. I've written a few books, and in recent years I've been teaching in Bible schools: in Manhattan with Michael Brown and then in Connecticut with Brian Simmons. But they both closed for various reasons. I now conduct a Bible study twice a month in my apartment in Astoria, and I'm an associate pastor in a small church in Queens. And on the weekdays I work for King Kullen Supermarkets in Long Island. I'm not sure what God has next for me, but I'm open to whatever He would have."

"What would you like to do? If you could describe what you'd enjoy the most, what would that be?"

"Well, Lynn and I both feel that church planting is behind us. I've really enjoyed teaching in Bible schools. I'd love to teach again in a school, especially one that's preparing students for the ministry."

Pastor Don stared at me, a stare of both shock and excitement. And then I heard the very same words I heard him say to me that began my life of pastoral ministry, way back in 1988. He slowly said, "Well, this is interesting."

"What is?"

"Do you even know that we started a Bible school here at Brooklyn Teen Challenge?" I shook my head no as he continued. "It's been going for about a year now. Any student who graduates the program and feels called to the ministry is offered one year of Bible college. We had two teachers, but one recently left; and we've been desperately looking for another teacher to take his place."

"Really?"

"Charles, if you want the job, it's yours. I don't even need a résumé! I know and trust you."

"When does your next semester start?"

"Tomorrow morning, at 9:00 A.M.!"

In June 2017, I celebrated six years of serving the Lord here at Brooklyn Teen Challenge, the original (flagship) Teen Challenge Center founded by David and Don Wilkerson in 1958. I now work here full-time as a teacher and a pastor. I'm so honored to work with Pastor Don once again, helping to continue the legacy of David Wilkerson.

I wish God would speak to me more often through divine dreams. It only occurs for me about three or four times a year. But when I receive one, there's no doubt as to the source and the message it contains. For instance, a few months after I began working here, I had a dream that I immediately knew was from the Lord.

In the dream, Pastor Don and I were standing on a street corner at night, less than a block away from Brooklyn Teen Challenge. We were there talking for most of the night. When the morning light began to fill the sky, Pastor Dave came out of a brownstone building, crossed the street close to us, and began to enter another building. I walked after him and caught up to him right before he entered. He turned and said, "Charles, didn't I tell you in the past that I don't like for people to stay up all night waiting up for me?"

"I didn't do that, Pastor Dave. I didn't even know you were around. Pastor Don and I were just up talking."

Pastor Dave then said to me, "The Lord says, 'Since you honor your elders without worshiping them and worshiping the way they did things, you have the ability to help Teen Challenge go to the next level in God without destroying its original DNA.'"

When I woke up, I realized that second-generation ministry leaders usually either drop the baton, keep a ministry at the very same level, or they destroy its DNA. Genuine spiritual sons can take it to the next level in God while maintaining its original vision and DNA. I got permission from Brother Don to buy lettering to paste on the large cafeteria wall here at the original Teen Challenge Center. It's a quote from Pastor Dave I first read on the subway (thirty-seven years ago in 1980!) from chapter 14 of *The Cross and the Switchblade*:

> "The house I had dreamed of, we might call it Teen Challenge Center: an atmosphere of discipline and affection. Christians living together, working together; a family." The dream lives on!

16

A Tribute to Don Wilkerson

IF DAVID WILKERSON IS A WORTHY EXAMPLE OF A FAITH-FILLED MAN OF God, then surely his younger brother Don is a shining example of a faithful man of God. His original call to ministry in New York City wasn't as dramatic as his brother's, but it was just as real. It came in the form of a phone call from his older brother David, asking him to come and help him! He's actually been as much of a spiritual father to me as Pastor Dave. Honestly, none of those giants Pastor Dave defeated were conquered alone. Pastor Don is the co-founder of both Teen Challenge and Times Square Church. I was very blessed to work alongside Brother Don in Manhattan and again at Brooklyn Teen Challenge. When Brother Don asked me to come on staff with him in Brooklyn, I told him that God was emphasizing the biblical message of sonship to my heart. Because of this, I have changed my life Scripture from Matthew 25 to Philippians 2:

> *His lord said to him, "Well done, good and faithful servant; you were faithful over a few things, I will make you ruler over many things. Enter into the joy of your lord"* (Matthew 25:21).

"But I trust in the Lord Jesus to send Timothy to you shortly...I have no one like-minded, who will sincerely care for your state...you know his proven character, that as a son with his father he served with me in the gospel" (Phil. 2:19-22).

In other words, I don't just want to be a faithful servant to God; I also desire to be a son—to my Heavenly Father and my earthly spiritual fathers—and to, in turn, be a father to others. (I have learned through the years, the fastest way to find a true spiritual father—like Paul was to Timothy—is to focus on pouring into the Timothys you can find all around you. Proverbs 11:25 says, *"He who waters will also be watered himself"* (NKJV). When Pastor Dave was building the ministry of Teen Challenge through traveling, speaking, and being in the limelight, his brother was faithfully holding down the fort in Brooklyn, day after day, year after year. In many ways, I can relate to Brother Don even more than Pastor Dave. As a young believer, the Lord gave me a promise: if I would be willing to play second fiddle, He would (spiritually) allow me to play in the best orchestras in the world. I have gladly served as an associate or as a staff member not only in Teen Challenge and Times Square Church, but also with Billy Graham's ministry, FIRE School of Ministry, Peter Wagner's School of Ministry, Brian Simmons, Joel Sadaphal, Vincent Buonfiglio, Gary Frost, Russell Hodgins, and others. Even so, the greatest second-fiddle-player trophy in Heaven surely is reserved for Don Wilkerson. And he'll gladly wait for that day when he'll be properly and eternally rewarded by God, instead of by fickle people.

One day, at the end of a service at Times Square Church, I was standing beside Brother Don as a lady came up to greet him. She screamed, "Oh my God! David Wilkerson! I'm so thrilled to finally meet you! Can you please sign this copy of *The Cross and the Switchblade* I just bought from the book table?"

Pastor Don politely replied, "I'm not David. I'm his brother, Don."

The lady gave him a mean look and said with deep disappointment, "Oh," and then walked away as though Brother Don just became invisible.

He knew I had just witnessed the whole thing, and he turned to me, smiled, and shrugged his shoulders. I'll never forget that smile. It said, "That's the thousandth time I've experienced that, but it's OK. God knows who I am, and that's enough for me." I'm grateful that throughout my entire adult life, Brother Don's cheerful smile, humble attitude, and wise counsel have always been there for me.

Epilogue

Famous and Not-So-Famous Quotes

I WILL ALWAYS TREASURE THE THINGS PASTOR DAVE TOLD ME PERSON-
ally, as well as the sermons I've heard him preach throughout the
years—from the message about Moses, Joshua, and Caleb in 1978
to the short exhortation he gave the last time I saw him at a pastors'
prayer meeting at Times Square Church a few years ago. I'd like to
share some of his most famous quotes and then reiterate the gems of
advice he gave me as one of his spiritual sons, along with the page
numbers where they're located:

> "As I look back over fifty years of ministry, I recall innu-
> merable tests, trials, and times of crushing pain. But
> through it all, the Lord has proven faithful, loving, and
> totally true to all His promises."

> "Stewards of the Gospel should be redeeming the time
> and not squandering so much of it on hobbies, sports,
> recreation, and television. Show me a man of God who
> sits before the TV idol, flitting away precious hours, vex-
> ing his soul and mind with the corruption of hell—and

I'll show you an unjust steward whom God will soon bring into account and strip of all spiritual authority."

"Some Christians are content to merely exist until they die. They don't want to risk anything, to believe God, to grow or mature. They refuse to believe His Word, and have become hardened in their unbelief. Now they're living just to die."

"How quickly we forget God's great deliverances in our lives. How easily we take for granted the miracles He performed in our past."

"Love is not only something you feel, it is something you do."

"You can have as much of Jesus as you want."

"It's all [our material things] gonna burn. You know what really matters? That we know Him!"

"Don't ever be a carbon copy of me. Instead, be a carbon copy of Jesus."

"Remember what my grandfather used to say. 'God always makes a way for a praying man.'"

"Many of those who once were so passionately in love with Christ now run about pursuing their own interests. They're burdened down with stress and problems, chasing after riches and the things of this world."

"Riches and the things that are necessary in life are not evil in themselves. And all of us face cares and troubles in this life. The sin comes in the time and energy we spend in pursuing these things, at the expense of neglecting Christ."

"Some of my suffering was self-imposed, caused by ignorance or foolishness. But now, at 74 years of age, I can boldly testify: never has God failed me."

"We have in our hands one of the prime theaters in America, and I think God says, 'If I can trust you with the poor, I can trust you with the Mark Hellinger.'"

"There are people having great emotional experiences right now and calling it revival. But I think true revival will come through searing, heart-piercing, convicting preaching where people are driven to their knees to repent."

"Jesus knows what it is like to be cheated on! He has been patient and long-suffering as all through history His beloved Israel has been unfaithful to Him, committing spiritual adultery over and over again. The heart of Jesus yearns for a faithful bride. How He longs for a people who will have eyes only for Him, with no other love coming between. What is it that brings joy to a wife or a husband? It is faithfulness—the ability to look into each other's eyes and see trust."

"You could cut me up into a thousand pieces and lay them in the street, and every piece will still love you."

"You can take it from this skinny preacher from the hills of Pennsylvania; the cross is mightier than the switchblade."[44]

And here's a few quotes Pastor Dave told me, or I personally heard him preach (already mentioned earlier, but worth repeating):

"Within that entire multitude of people who came out of Egypt with Moses, only two men followed the Lord with all their hearts—Joshua and Caleb. Because they were sold out to God, they were given supernatural courage!" (pg. 25)

"When you have authority, you don't have to yell" (pg. 72).

"Don't ever make major decisions when you're sick, depressed, or worn out" (pg. 94).

"The need can indicate a call, but it is not to dictate the call. The prodigal son found himself in a place where no man helped him so he would look up to Heaven for help. We need to differentiate between our calling and the needs of the people around us. And no one is called to meet every need he sees" (pg. 95).

"If you don't hear clearly from the Lord whom to marry, this could destroy the calling on your life" (pg. 103).

"Beloved, there are times when staying in God's presence is more important than getting enough sleep, getting enough to eat, or getting enough of anything else" (pg. 104).

"Trust what you hear when you're in God's presence. Doubt what you hear when your heart is filled with fears and anxieties" (pg. 105).

"I don't believe in long marriage engagements. When you know it's God, why wait? Waiting too long just puts you in hard situations" (pg. 111).

"Here's my [marriage counseling] advice. Have a lot of mercy on each other, especially for the first year. When you have disputes, just say, 'I'll have mercy on you if you'll have mercy on me'" (pg. 111).

"No matter how strong an Old Testament prophet's message was, it always included words of hope and encouragement. So we need to do the same" (pg. 118).

"Don't ever try to be anointed. Just try to meet the needs of the people you're ministering to, and the Lord will anoint you to do that. The anointing is to meet needs, and not for a show" (pg. 118).

"[God's] gifts are given to meet people's needs, not to create a circus atmosphere" (pg. 119).

"If you preach more than forty to forty-five minutes, you're going to lose the people. The fastest way to ruin a good sermon is to go a little too long. If you can't make your point in forty minutes, give it up!" (pg. 119)

"A father's ceiling should be his children's floor" (pg. 120).

"Don't become overly frustrated with all the shortcomings of God's people" (pg. 121).

"When you're willing to serve the servants, that's when heavenly promotion comes. Joseph gladly ministered to Pharaoh's servants in that awful prison, and before he knew it, he was in charge of all of Egypt" (pg. 130).

"A sanctified imagination is one of the mightiest weapons in the hands of God. If you want your sermons to become riveting, become addicted to reading, not to watching television" (pg. 130).

"God will bless you tremendously if He can trust you" (pg. 130).

"Don't get caught up in the numbers game, always striving for a bigger and better ministry. So many young pastors are consumed with packing the people in, but that kind of striving never ends. Bigger is not always better. Be content with what God gives you" (pg. 130).

"It's almost impossible to put too many Scriptures in a sermon. It's the power of God's Word that breaks hardened hearts. Allow conviction to go deep into people's hearts before you pull the scalpel out. Scripture-filled, convicting sermons are like successful heart surgeries: they save lives" (pg. 130).

"I don't care about it [the honor of man] for me, but I care about it for them. You can't lead people into the rich things of God if they don't honor you. It takes years to build a life of honor and just a few minutes of folly to lose it" (pg. 131).

"If you hunger for more of God, if you want Him to lay hold of your life, there is a price!" (pg. 156)

"When the Lord touches someone, that person is driven to his knees. He then becomes intimate with Christ. And out of that intimacy, he receives fresh revelation from Heaven" (pg. 161).

"God, wake us up! Let some of us get so hungry to be touched by Your hand, so set on fire and burdened for Your will and purposes, that You will come forth and pour out Your Spirit mightily!" (pg. 161)

"If you set your heart to pray, God's going to come and start sharing His heart with you" (pg. 161).

Along with his quotes and sermons, Pastor Dave's life spoke a strong and powerful message, showing us how we can walk in the footsteps of a man who accomplished great things for the Kingdom of God, and touched millions of people. By the grace and power of God, let's follow in his footsteps!

"And through his faith, though he died, he still speaks" (Hebrews 11:4 ESV).

Notes

1. Feet of clay: "(idiomatic) In someone apparently strong and without failings, a hidden weakness which could cause his or her downfall.... Used in the Bible in Daniel 2:34, part of the description of the huge statue in the dream of Chaldean King Nebuchadnezzar." See "Feet of Clay," *YourDictionary.com*, http://www.yourdictionary.com/feet-of-clay.

2. Gary Wilkerson, David's oldest son, published a great biography of his dad's life entitled *The Cross, the Switchblade, and the Man Who Believed*.

3. Keith Green, "Why YOU Should Go to the Mission Field," *Last Days Ministries*, February 22, 2007, http://www.lastdaysministries.org/Articles/1000008651/Last_Days_Ministries/LDM/Discipleship_Teachings/Keith_Green/Why_YOU_Should.aspx.

4. David Wilkerson, *The Cross and the Switchblade* (Grand Rapids, MI: Chosen Books, 1963), 137.

5. Ibid.

6. Ibid.

7. *"And I saw a great white throne and the One sitting on it. The earth and sky fled from His presence, but they found no place to hide"* (Rev. 20:11 NLT).

8. *"How is it then, brethren? Whenever you come together, each of you has a psalm, has a teaching, has a tongue, has a revelation, has an interpretation. Let all things be done for edification. If anyone speaks in a tongue, let there be two or at the most three, each in turn, and let one interpret. But if there is no interpreter, let him keep silent in church, and*

let him speak to himself and to God. Let two or three prophets speak, and let the others judge. But if anything is revealed to another who sits by, let the first keep silent. For you can all prophesy one by one, that all may learn and all may be encouraged. And the spirits of the prophets are subject to the prophets. For God is not the author of confusion but of peace, as in all the churches of the saints" (1 Cor. 14:26-33).

9. *"And her prophets have daubed them with untempered morter, seeing vanity, and divining lies unto them, saying, Thus saith the Lord God, when the Lord hath not spoken"* (Ezek. 22:28 KJV). *"But the prophet, which shall presume to speak a word in My name, which I have not commanded him to speak, or that shall speak in the name of other gods, even that prophet shall die"* (Deut. 18:20 KJV).

10. *"Let two or three prophets speak, and let the others judge"* (1 Cor. 14:29).

11. *"...in the days of His flesh, when He had offered up prayers and supplications with strong crying and tears unto Him that was able to save Him from death, and was heard in that He feared"* (Heb. 5:7 KJV).

12. *"'Abba, Father,' He cried out, 'everything is possible for You. Please take this cup of suffering away from Me. Yet I want Your will to be done, not Mine'"* (Mark 14:36 NLT).

13. *"This left Jacob all alone in the camp, and a man came and wrestled with him until the dawn began to break. When the man saw that he would not win the match, he touched Jacob's hip and wrenched it out of its socket. Then the man said, 'Let me go, for the dawn is breaking!' But Jacob said, 'I will not let you go unless you bless me.' 'What is your name?' the man asked. He replied, 'Jacob.' 'Your name will no longer be Jacob,' the man told him. 'From now on you will be called Israel, because you have fought with God and with men and have won'"* (Gen. 32:24-28 NLT).

14. *"The fear of man brings a snare, but whoever trusts in the Lord shall be safe"* (Prov. 29:25).

15. *"And Gideon built an altar to the Lord there and named it Yahweh-Shalom (which means, 'the Lord is peace')"* (Judg. 6:24a NLT).

16. *"This charge I commit to you, son Timothy, according to the prophecies previously made concerning you, that by them you may wage the good warfare"* (1 Tim. 1:18).

17. *"And when they were come up out of the water, the Spirit of the Lord caught away Philip, that the eunuch saw him no more: and he went on his way rejoicing"* (Acts 8:39 KJV).

18. *"Therefore they shall come and sing in the height of Zion, and shall flow together to the goodness of the Lord..."* (Jer. 31:12 KJV).

19. Leonard Ravenhill, *Revival God's Way: A Message for the Church* (Bethany House, 1983), pg. 32 .

20. *"For God may speak in one way, or in another, yet man does not perceive it. In a dream, in a vision of the night, when deep sleep falls upon men, while slumbering on their beds, then He opens the ears of men, and seals their instruction"* (Job 33:14-16).

21. *"My people ask counsel from their wooden idols, and their staff informs them. For the spirit of harlotry has caused them to stray, and they have played the harlot against their God"* (Hosea 4:12).

22. *"The manifestation of the Spirit is given to each one for the profit of all: for to one is given the word of wisdom through the Spirit, to another the word of knowledge through the same Spirit, to another faith by the same Spirit, to another gifts of healings by the same Spirit, to another the working of miracles, to another prophecy, to another discerning of spirits, to another different kinds of tongues, to another the interpretation of tongues"* (1 Cor. 12:7-10).

23. *"...You will show me the path of life: in Your presence is fullness of joy; at Your right hand are pleasures forevermore"* (Ps. 16:11).

24. *"Also, anoint Jehu son of Nimshi king over Israel, and anoint Elisha son of Shaphat from Abel Meholah to succeed you as prophet.... So Elijah went from there and found Elisha son of Shaphat. He was plowing with twelve yoke of oxen, and he himself was driving the twelfth pair. Elijah went up to him and threw his cloak around him...then he set out to follow Elijah and became his servant"* (1 Kings 19:16,19,21 NIV).

25. *"And so it was, when they had crossed over, that Elijah said to Elisha, 'Ask! What may I do for you, before I am taken away from you?' Elisha said, 'Please let a double portion of your spirit be upon me.' So he said, 'You have asked a hard thing. Nevertheless, if you see me when I am taken from you, it shall be so for you; but if not, it shall not be so'"* (2 Kings 2:9-10).

26. *"When a prophet speaks in the name of the Lord, if the thing does not happen or come to pass, that is the thing which the Lord has not spoken; the prophet has spoken it presumptuously; you shall not be afraid of him"* (Deut. 18:22).

27. *"Is anyone among you sick? Let him call for the elders of the church, and let them pray over him, anointing him with oil in the name of the Lord. And the prayer of faith will save the sick, and the Lord will raise him up..."* (James 5:14-15).

28. *"Then he prepared a great feast for them; and after they ate and drank, he sent them away and they went to their master. So the bands of Syrian raiders came no more into the land of Israel"* (2 Kings 6:23).

29. *"Pure and undefiled religion before God and the Father is this: to visit orphans and widows in their trouble, and to keep oneself unspotted from the world"* (James 1:27).

30. *"To the church of God which is at Corinth, to those who are sanctified in Christ Jesus, called to be saints, with all who in every place call on the name of Jesus Christ our Lord, both theirs and ours"* (1 Cor. 1:2).

31. Mack Tomlinson, *In Light of Eternity: The Life of Leonard Ravenhill* (Lion Share Books, 2010), Kindle edition, chap. 31.

32. *"And the father of circumcision to those who not only are of the circumcision, but who also walk in the steps of the faith which our father Abraham had while still uncircumcised...the promise might be sure to all the seed, not only to those who are of the law, but also to those who are of the faith of Abraham, who is the father of us all"* (Rom. 4:12,16).

33. Pastor Dave's sermons can be found at http://www.worldchallenge.org.

34. *"Is not this the fast that I have chosen? To loose the bands of wickedness, to undo the heavy burdens, and to let the oppressed go free, and that ye break every yoke? Is it not to deal thy bread to the hungry, and that thou bring the poor that are cast out to thy house? when thou seest the naked, that thou cover him; and that thou hide not thyself from thine own flesh?"* (Isa. 58:6 KJV).

35. David Wilkerson, "The Touch of God" (sermon, Times Square Church, New York, NY, August 5, 1991).

36. "The History of Times Square Church," *Tscnyc.com*, http://www.tscnyc.org/history/.

37. David Wilkerson, "The Touch of God."

38. David Wilkerson, "The Queen in Gold! The Bride of Christ" (sermon, Times Square Church, New York, NY, March 13, 1995).

39. Gary Wilkerson, *David Wilkerson: The Cross, the Switchblade, and the Man Who Believed* (Grand Rapids, MI: Zondervan, 2014), 250-51.

40. Don Wilkerson, "Going into Labor" (Sermon, Teen Challenge, Brooklyn, NY, March 9, 2016).

41. David Wilkerson, "The Touch of God."

42. David Wilkerson, "A Call to Anguish" (sermon, Times Square Church, New York, NY, September 15, 2002), www.sermonindex.net.

43. David Wilkerson, *The Cross and the Switchblade*, 137.

44. These quotes and more can be found in David Wilkerson's sermons and writings, many of which are collected on the World Challenge website, http://worldchallenge.org.

About the Author

CHARLES SIMPSON, THE ELEVENTH OF TWELVE CHILDREN, WAS BORN and raised in Tennessee. After his conversion at the age of seventeen, he received a missionary call to New York City, where he has spent most of his adult life, pastoring, planting churches, and working in Bible schools. While serving as the pastor of prayer at Times Square Church, he met and married his wife, Lynn. They have been privileged to work alongside great leaders such as David and Don Wilkerson, Michael Brown, Peter Wagner, Brian Simmons, Vincent Buonfiglio, Joel Sadaphal, Russell Hodgins, and Will Kitchen. Charles served as the campus pastor at Brooklyn Teen Challenge and the director of its School of Ministry, and is currently planting his sixth church (www.oasislic.com).

FREE E-BOOKS?
YES, PLEASE!

Get **FREE** and deeply discounted **Christian books** for your **e-reader** delivered to your inbox **every week!**

IT'S SIMPLE!

VISIT lovetoreadclub.com

SUBSCRIBE by entering your email address

RECEIVE free and discounted e-book offers and inspiring articles delivered to your inbox every week!

Unsubscribe at any time.

SUBSCRIBE NOW!

LOVE TO READ CLUB

visit **LOVETOREADCLUB.COM** ▶